LF

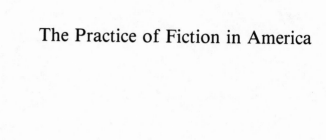

The Practice of Fiction in America

The Practice of Fiction in America:

Writers from Hawthorne to the Present

JEROME KLINKOWITZ

The Iowa State University Press, Ames

to my Mother, Lucille McNamara Klinkowitz

and to the memory of my Father, Jerome F. Klinkowitz, Sr.

JEROME KLINKOWITZ is Professor of English at the University of Northern Iowa, and is the author of *Literary Disruptions* (1975, revised and expanded 1980) and *The Life of Fiction* (1977); coauthor of *The Vonnegut Statement* (1973) and *Vonnegut in America* (1977); compiler of bibliographies of Kurt Vonnegut (1974) and Donald Barthelme (1977); and editor of *Innovative Fiction* (1972), *Writing Under Fire: Stories of the Vietnam War* (1978), and *The Diaries of Willard Motley* (1979). His essays have appeared in *The Nation, The New Republic, The Village Voice, Partisan Review,* and in many scholarly journals around the world.

Composed and printed by The Iowa State University Press, Ames, Iowa 50010
No part of this publication may be reproduced, stored in a retrieval system, or transmitted, in any form or by any means, electronic, mechanical, photocopying, recording, or otherwise, without prior written permission of the publisher.

First edition, 1980

Library of Congress Cataloging in Publication Data

Klinkowitz, Jerome.
   The practice of fiction in America.

   Includes bibliographical references and index.
     1. American fiction—History and criticism.
I. Title.
PS371.K55   813 .009   80–13608
ISBN 0–8138–1420–0

C O N T E N T S

vi

PREFACE

THE PROVOCATION to write this book comes from the Uniwersytet Maria Curie-Skłowskiej in Lublin, Poland, where I was invited to give several lectures in 1979, and from a shorter set of lectures and discussions at the Centre de Recherche sur la Littérature Américaine Contemporaine de l'Université de Paris III (Sorbonne Nouvelle) in the Spring. Such international perspective on my perhaps chauvinistically American thesis proved to be beneficial, and to Professors Jerzy Kutnik and André Le Vot I am especially grateful.

The editors of *ESQ: Journal of the American Renaissance, Modern Fiction Studies, Critique, Proof, Players, The New Republic,* and *Forms of the American Imagination* (Institut für Amerikanistik, der Universität Innsbruck) published parts of my commentary on Hawthorne, Howells, Faulkner, Motley, Vonnegut, and Updike in different form, and I am grateful for their permission to redo that material here. The chapters on Kate Chopin, Scott Fitzgerald, and Donald Barthelme, plus the Prologue and Epilogue were written originally for this volume.

The University of Northern Iowa and its Department of English Language and Literature have been generous funding my work, including several research grants. In a day of slim support for the Humanities, President John Kamerick, Vice-President and Provost James G. Martin, Deans H. Ray Hoops and Margarette Eby, and Chairmen Jan Robbins and Daniel Cahill have distinguished themselves by their strong commitment to the adequate funding of research, and deserve thanks from every scholar fortunate enough to work at the University in Cedar Falls.

JEROME KLINKOWITZ

Cedar Falls, Iowa /Lublin, Poland
June /October, 1979

The Practice of Fiction in America

The Practice of Fiction in America

IN A SENSE, all American fiction is experimental. In England the eighteenth century novel, that wonderfully variegated genre that did virtually everything possible with prose, soon withdrew into the nineteenth century novel of manners, and but for a few exceptions like *Wuthering Heights* and *The Way of All Flesh* spent generation after generation mirroring the stable middle-class life of its most faithful readership.

America, of course, has prided itself from the start as a classless society, where manners were secondary to morals and lords and ladies (as models to the bourgeoisie) did not exist. Significantly, the novel of manners did not thrive in this country until after the Civil War, when business and manufacturing expansion produced a cynically named privileged class: the robber barons and railroad kings of the 1870s, 1880s, and 1890s. But even then our writers saw their chance for literary experiment, as William Dean Howells and others set off upon a road to realism which would be a decidedly aesthetic journey.

From the start, the unique conditions of American life forced our writers into new and strikingly original modes. Because his own literary devices were so atypical, Nathaniel Hawthorne found it impossible to begin a book without a disclaiming preface. What America offered was as elusive and ethereal as the speculative conditions of its own political founding. Washington Irving before him and Henry James soon after chose travel and literary exile in Europe and England rather than staying home and forcing the unyielding American materials into foreign stereotypes of form. Even in the twentieth century T. S. Eliot and Ezra Pound preferred London and Paris for the shaping of modernism, and the latter city persisted as the obligatory Mecca for the Lost Generation. It was the writers who stayed home, however, who wrote the most characteristically imaginative fiction. Like the Constitution and the Bill

3

of Rights, their works have proven to be original and lasting documents, basing themselves less on social experience than on projective imaginative power. From the spiritual dreams of the Puritan founders through the civic idealism of the Founding Fathers down to the zealots of Manifest Destiny, Americans have been a peculiarly visionary people. Few countries can claim such a strongly fanciful heritage. America is imagination's own land.

Imaginative latitude of fashion and material are what Hawthorne claimed for his own work. His Preface to *The House of the Seven Gables* (1851) argued against the solid beef-and-ale realities of British social fiction and preferred instead the subtler tints and more evanescent flavor of American life. But the differences ran deeper than Hawthorne could anticipate, creating a major problem with form which was to tax his artistic strength. More influenced by the novel of manners than he chose to realize, Hawthorne was distressed by the unhappy endings fated for his American romances. Spurred on by the complaints of his wife, of his favorite literary critic (E. P. Whipple), and of his own conscience, he struggled to contradict the inexorable tendency of his own material. The laboratory for his experiment was his second full-length romance. Begun as a typically Hawthornesque meditation, *The House of the Seven Gables* ends as a well-made novel of manners with a happy resolution for all. Its failure, however, indicates the strength of Hawthorne's other works and establishes an essential principle for the development of American fiction: self-conscious critical attention to matters of theme and form will be the yardstick by which our fiction grows.

By the time of William Dean Howells, in the next generation of American fictionists, the novel itself was the center of a major aesthetic battle between the elder genteel idealists (representing New England transcendentalism in its decline) and the younger socially committed writers from the West. How to locate his writing in reality yet still maintain aesthetic order was Howells' first test. His career began with travel literature based on his and Mrs. Howells' time in Venice (where Howells was American consul, a political favor earned by his campaign biography of Lincoln). Soon afterward his first novel, *Their Wedding Journey* (1872), invented two fictional stand-ins (Basil and Isabel March) but still relied on travelogue to fill out the action. What makes the novel interesting is Howells' running debate on the subject of ethics and aesthetics—the socially pertinent subject of what the author considered responsible fiction pitted against the sentimental tide of aesthetics (at this point Idealism in decay). Howells stayed with this topic, and with these two characters so close to his own emotional life, throughout the next three decades. By the century's end he had expanded and matured their voyeuristic sentimentalism into self-responsible creativity; as Basil and Isabel March grew as characters, Howells learned and expressed more about how fiction and experience intermesh. Less of a successfully self-conscious critic, Mark Twain spent the last decade of his life wrestling with similar problems—and being destroyed by them. Yet each writer was on to something important. In the process, their own fiction more and more resembled the modern novel.

But first came the experiment with literary naturalism. Emile Zola had introduced the style and the name for it in France with his essay "The Experimental Novel." *Experimental* was used in the clinical rather than aesthetic sense; characters in a novel were to be studied like rats in a maze, and like variables in a controlled experiment would tell the author and reader more about the scientific laws which were assumed to govern life. The first American imitations of Zola's method were heavy-handed and are best read today as parodies. Frank Norris was a master of Zola's formula, and hence his novels are formulaic—*McTeague* (1899) moving toward its conclusion like a machine winding down, while *Vandover and the Brute* (written ca. 1895) is even more apparent in its pathological thesis.

How naturalism, seemingly a step backward in the development of fiction, would find its way to modernism can be seen from a striking literary experiment by Kate Chopin, her novel *The Awakening* (1899). Most Americanized naturalism would begin with a thesis and then follow it through the action to the inexorable and forewarned conclusion. An explicitly deductive method, it contradicted the spirit of Zola's belief and made for boring, reductive literature. Kate Chopin's success was to take the essentials of the naturalistic process and imbed them in the texture of her novel. Inductive rather than deductive, the story is a process of discovery for her heroine as she "awakens" to certain natural urges not conventionally treated in novels by women before. Discovery is made part of the reader's experience by virtue of a carefully composed set of images. Unlike Norris, who explains his behavioral science directly, Kate Chopin weaves it into her imagery. We hear less of physical symptoms and more of the seductiveness of the sea, a persistent image which reaches back to the heroine's youth. All the essentials of naturalism are incorporated in *The Awakening,* but as literary rather than scientific metaphors. Compositional integrity rather than scientific principle determines how the novel is written, and as a result it is as readable today as it was eighty years ago.

F. Scott Fitzgerald used the same control of imagery to grow from a nineteenth century novelist to a modernist master in just five years. His first book, *This Side of Paradise* (1920), ignored many of Henry James' selectivist innovations and held more closely to H. G. Wells' reactionary "novel of saturation," a way of writing which placed the highest premium on artistically uncorrupted experience. Naturalistic determination need not be a feature, but most other elements from this reductive style of fiction prevailed, including strict chronology, historically detailed characterization, and a disinclination to shape experience or select events for aesthetic coherence. Fitzgerald's subject, the life and loves of a Princeton sophomore named Amory Blaine, appeared suited to this history-laden technique. The strategy works until Fitzgerald tries to make a point. Such artistic interference, necessary to the work of a twentieth century novelist but so alien to the novel of saturation, makes the book fall apart in his hands. The omniscient narrator becomes as befuddled as his adolescent moon-struck character, and the narrative becomes a shambles. Fitzgerald flirts with the same danger in *The Great Gatsby* (1925), but with the tools of artistic selection and commentary through imagery—Kate Chopin's lesson—he manages to make his narrator's momentary infatuation an essential part of the novel's action. Nick Carraway assembles and sorts out the action as a way of perceiving Jay Gatsby; a highly selective and artificial novel is thus written before our eyes in a most credible manner. Fitzgerald has given twentieth century art its most unique gift, the benefit of having it both ways.

That thematics could profit from the same compositional design was shown again by William Faulkner, whose multivolumed epic of Yoknapatawpha County proved to be one continuous novel written over thirty-four years. Theme as controlling vision is most apparent in Faulkner's only fully integrated collection of short fiction, *Knight's Gambit* (1949). Though supposedly detective stories centered about the life of Gavin Stevens, *Knight's Gambit* shows itself to be a more profound meditation on the theme of community. The various stories point to different aspects: insiders, outsiders, natives, and outlanders, with the ratiocination and detection merely a formal excuse to introduce the theme. In no sense are the thematics simple rehearsals of history; instead, the single story of Yoknapatawpha's residents and aliens is told and retold from a multitude of different angles, until by the book's end Faulkner has achieved in miniature an effect not unlike that of his whole Yoknapatawpha saga.

A great irony in the development of American fiction is that an entire decade of concern was directed to the social use of fiction, a debate once hopefully concluded by William Dean Howells but which during the Great Depression once again became the novel's matter of concern, with no major gain of innovations in theme or form. The thirties were the years of Faulkner's most brilliant and prolific efforts, but for him thematics were an aesthetic concern. At the other extreme proletarian novelists such as Jack Conroy and Tom Kromer were so heavily committed to social reform that critics judged their art a distraction. The major writers to emerge from this decade—John Steinbeck and John O'Hara— soon retreated into the elegantly crafted novel of manners, preparing the way for such later stylists as John Updike and John Cheever but adding little to the progress of fiction in their time.

Steinbeck's major contribution was a highly commercial house style which has persisted in best-sellers down to our own day. The case of Willard Motley, writing socially self-conscious fiction in the 1940s but still edited and told to rewrite his material according to the aesthetics of Steinbeck, James T. Farrell, and Richard Wright, illustrates what happens when a potentially major writer is not allowed to be his own best critic but is instead maneuvered into repeating stylistic successes of the past. Motley's unpublished manuscripts and the passages cut from his published novel *Knock on Any Door* (1947) suggest that he was anticipating a phenomenological spirit of new realism, and that in his social interest he was a deconstructionist who would substitute fictional models for unhappy social affairs. Had he been edited by the Paris intellectuals at Editions de Minuit, who gave the world Alain Robbe-Grillet and the *nouveau roman,* instead of by the businessmen who ran Macmillan and Appleton-Century in the postwar years, Willard Motley and his decade of apprenticeship might now be considered a revolutionary and innovative period for American fiction, instead of the backwater we now judge it to have been.

Most serious American writers since the 1950s have been affected by the realism debate. Some, like Bernard Malamud, have substituted the secular mythology of Jewish-American urban life for the deeper symbology of the modernists. Others, most notably Saul Bellow, have moved directly to the exposition of morality, to the extent that some accuse Bellow of bypassing fiction entirely for essays, conversations, and debates. At the opposite extreme has been John Updike, whose own lush stylistic sensuosity at times obscures his story's action. Such an overbalance of the stylistic, it is claimed, creates literary decadence; having nothing to write about, Updike writes anyway, his lack of substance disguised by a thick sauce of adjectives, adverbs, and nouns.

What Updike has in fact accomplished is the legitimate use of writing as its own subject. From the start he has been careful to have his theme justify his stylistic excesses: the baroque obsolescence of the old folks in *The Poorhouse Fair* (1959), his protagonist's erotic aestheticism in *Rabbit, Run* (1960), and the self-conscious sensuality rampant throughout his most controversial novel, *Couples* (1968). Originally a master of light verse, capable of writing Pindaric odes on the qualities of a cough drop, Updike has matured as a stylist who makes the act of writing itself perform the major action of his novel.

An entirely different way of dealing with reality has been perfected by Kurt Vonnegut. Challenged by the bleakly pessimistic view of life he encountered during World War II and again in the postwar corporate economy, Vonnegut drew on his anthropological training to decide that no single view of the world can claim precedence over any other—that reality itself is simply a description, and that the legitimacy of any one account depends solely upon how persuasively that account is stated. That is, of course, the practice of the fictionist, and Vonnegut soon learned how to discredit assumed notions of reality by demonstrating their arbitrary and conventional nature and then substituting a more effective description of his own. From *Player Piano* (1952) through *Slaughterhouse-Five* (1969) Vonnegut consumed and regenerated the main aspects of our culture, from individual human worth to the notion of free will. That his talent was tied to the practice of fiction is proven by his single experiment in legitimate theatre, the Broadway play *Happy Birthday, Wanda June* (1970–71). Here the different axioms of dramatic art caused his vision to be readjusted without notable success. But once returned to fiction, the Vonnegut magic reassumed its transformative power.

The breakthrough in American fiction came in the late 1960s and early 1970s, when an erratically brilliant group of young fictionists attacked social realism in its own grounds, and then proposed in its place a fiction whose prime feature would be its own physical structure of words, sentences, and paragraphs. The first novels by these innovationists were wildly comic and sexually exuberant affairs, such as Ronald Sukenick's *Up* (1968), Donald Barthelme's *Snow White* (1967), and Steve Katz's *The Exagggerations of Peter Prince* (1968). A great deal of deconstruction was necessary, including devices which would strip away the illusion of reality and substitute the self-conscious honesty of the writer writing his or her story. Beneath this new convention of throwing out conventions lay the mature work of innovative fiction, where writers such as Donald Barthelme and Richard Brautigan would take the common reader's familiar notions about language (from television, advertising, and vernacular speech) and exploit their objecthood. Barthelme's models were the collage method of Max Ernst and the assemblages of Joseph Cornell; in each case the artist could use objects as factors in his composition without sacrificing their real identity as artifacts preexisting his work. The central challenge of fiction, that unlike daubs of paint or notes of music words bring with them their own universe of previous references and associations, spurred the best of these new writers toward finding ways of keeping language on the page as artifact. The results have been hysterically comic (Gilbert Sorrentino's *Imaginative Qualities of Actual Things,* 1971), typographically bizarre (Raymond Federman's *Double or Nothing,* 1971), and deeply lyrical (Clarence Major's *Emergency Exit,* 1979). Helpful outlines of this new aesthetic have been supplied by Sukenick, Federman, Sorrentino, William H. Gass, and many other practicing fictionists. Indeed, the new fictionists must be their own aesthetic theorists, a practice common to all major developments in American writing.

American writers have been especially responsive to critical problems in their work since its beginning. What starts as outside criticism—Edwin P. Whipple to Hawthorne, Alfred Kazin to Barthelme—soon becomes the most exacting self-criticism. An awareness of problems in literary form, therefore, from the beginnings of serious American fiction down to today's avant-garde, has described the course of our literary heritage. The practice of fiction in America has been a necessarily self-conscious affair, for the challenges each writer faces have led in almost dialectical fashion to the next style of writing—hence the succession of major styles from Hawthorne's day to the present. This very self-consciousness has contributed to its greatness, for in facing these critical problems American authors have in turn produced their finest, most characteristic, and most innovative writing. The integrity of their finished work was foremost on these writers' minds; the sometimes painful awareness of threats to that integrity often made their final products masterpieces.

Hawthorne's Sense of an Ending

PARTIALLY through myth but largely by his own self-conscious behavior, Nathaniel Hawthorne has become an archetype for the troubled American artist. From his journals we know that themes of guilt and responsibility rattled his mind, and—if we are to believe his biographers—the very attempt to write, to "open an intercourse with the outside world," unsettled his soul. A quick look at the three most famous portraits of him—by Charles Osgood in 1840 (age thirty-six), George P. A. Healey in 1852 (age forty-eight), and most strikingly by the British photographer Mayall in 1860 (age fifty-six)—reveals an interior aging process not unlike that of Oscar Wilde's picture of Dorian Gray. Osgood's portrait shows Hawthorne looking not a day over twenty-one; twelve years' solitude, culminating with *Twice-Told Tales,* had been no psychic burden, and had left him quite the young man who'd graduated from Bowdoin in 1825. But Healey's Hawthorne, the veteran of three major romances (the term he preferred for booklength fictions), is a driven man. The hairline has receded to reveal a troubled brow, the hair itself is now frayed and pulled, and the eyes seem as if dazed by the ponderous complexities of *The Scarlet Letter, The House of the Seven Gables,* and *The Blithedale Romance.* But the worst was yet to come. The Mayall photo is devastating: a man aged thirty years in less than a decade, worn down by *The Marble Faun* and facing four unfinishable romances, the struggles of his artistic life seemingly come to naught. A fourth portrait, by Matthew Brady in 1863, shows an old and broken man.

Writing romances obviously took its toll on Hawthorne's person, but his artistic powers were more specifically taxed as he struggled to write a book with a happy ending. To his own mind, he succeeded with Holgrave and Phoebe in *The House of the Seven Gables,* but the ending to that work remains, after a century and more of critical bickering, a controversial topic. Newton Arvin was not the first to call it "inorganic";[1] Hawthorne's own favorite critic, Edwin Percy Whipple, made the same accusation, as did Evert Duyckinck in the book's first major review.[2] To defend the ending, commentators have turned to the facts of biography and the theory of romance, while detractors have claimed that Hawthorne, in his third novel, was already disintegrating as an artist.[3] What has not been done, however, is to compare the endings of all five completed romances, which are remarkably similar in theme. Holgrave and Phoebe's love, so anomalous when viewed by itself, is in fact a resolution Hawthorne considers in each of his romances from the collegiate *Fanshawe* to *The Marble Faun.* Throughout he demonstrates a great consistency, with the controversial ending serving as a variation on the theme of history's power in such romantic situations.

The matter of his third romance's resolution had, in fact, been with Hawthorne for most of his artistic career. When Holgrave falls in love, on an evening "So sweetly cool . . . that the summer Eve might be fancied as sprinkling dews and liquid moonlight, with a dash of icy temper in them, out of a silver vase," one recalls the silver vase and refreshing dew of "Dr. Heidegger's Experiment," published fourteen years earlier. It makes Holgrave feel "what he sometimes almost forgot, thrust so early, as he had been, into the rude struggle with man—how youthful he was."[4] Like the people in the doctor's experiment, he is transformed and sees the earth transformed with him, remarking that could he sustain the feeling, "the garden would every day be virgin soil . . . and the house!—it would be like a bower in Eden, blossoming with the earliest roses that God ever made" (II, 214). Holgrave is able to redefine his political logic, and effect a compromise with time, precisely because he is able to sustain such a vision. Holgrave and Phoebe keep the feelings which first possess them, and "They transfigured the earth, and made it Eden again" (II, 307). With such powers they can remove the Pyncheon curse and defeat the otherwise inexorable force of time.

The endings of Hawthorne's other romances present lovers in similar situations, but their love does not so easily resolve the conflicts which have preceded. When in *Fanshawe* the hero faces the prospect of life with Ellen Langton, we are told "It is impossible to conceive the flood of momentary joy, which the bare admission of such a possibility sent through his frame." But it is a case of "strong affections" rising "against reason" (III, 456). Fanshawe realizes at once that his joy "contained no mixture of hope, it had no reference to the future—it was the perfect bliss of a moment—an insulated point of happiness" (III, 452). The ending is responsible to historical fact: the sickly scholar wisely chooses to stay with his books, while the vivacious Ellen is bequeathed to the more suitable Edward Walcott.

In the forest scene of *The Scarlet Letter,* Hawthorne offers a similar treatment of the momentary power of love. Repeating their vows of fidelity and hoping to escape the claims of their socially constricting situation, Dimmesdale and Hester are propelled backwards to the joy of their youth. "The decision once made" to flee their past, Dimmesdale experiences "the exhilarating effect" common to "a prisoner just escaped from the dungeon of his own heart," and exclaims that he is a new man, "risen up all made anew" (I, 201-2). Hester loosens her hair, revives her complexion, and sees that "Her sex, her youth, and the whole richness of her beauty, came back from what men call the irrevocable past, and clustered themselves, with her maiden hope, and a happiness before unknown, within the magic circle of this hour" (I, 202). As she is transfigured, the earth itself harmonizes with her new emotion:

And, as if the gloom of the earth and sky had been but the effluence of these two mortal hearts, it vanished with their sorrow. All at once, as with a sudden smile of heaven, forth burst the sunshine, pouring a very flood into the obscure forest, gladdening each green leaf, transmuting the yellow fallen ones to gold, and gleaming adown the gray trunks of the solemn trees. (I, 202-3)

"Such was the sympathy of Nature," Hawthorne notes. "Love, whether newly born, or aroused from a death-like slumber, must always create a sunshine, filling the heart so full of radiance, that it overflows upon the outward world." As happens with Holgrave and Phoebe, Hester's and Dimmesdale's love transfigures the world. Indeed, "Had the forest still kept its gloom, it would have been bright in Hester's eyes, and bright in Arthur Dimmesdale's!" (I, 203). But as soon as we step back, we find that the lovers' vision is subjective and transitory. The context does not change; it is still "the great black forest" (I, 204) that it has been all along. The world still threatens their happiness, and they can neither escape their situation nor transform it into something it is not.

The integrity of *The Scarlet Letter*'s resolution is underscored by the chapter "The Child at the Brookside." In the moment of bliss preceding this chapter Hester has removed her scarlet letter, feeling an emotional release which has subjectively colored her vision of both nature and society. But little Pearl, as the concrete issue of her sin, demands the return of the outward sign of her mother's responsibility and limitation. With a child's insight for simple consistency and order, Pearl points her finger at Hester's bosom and commands, "Come thou and take it up!"

(I, 210). With "a sense of inevitable doom" Hester reassumes the letter; "her beauty, the warmth and richness of her womanhood, departed, like fading sunshine; and a gray shadow seemed to fall across her" (I, 211). In *The Scarlet Letter,* lovers may not escape the past as easily as do Holgrave and Phoebe. Perhaps Hester and Dimmesdale have hope for an "immortal life together" (I, 256), but in the temporal sphere the demands of history must be met.

In *The Blithedale Romance,* the utopian community is itself one moment of bliss writ large. As the idealistic projection of an altruistic society, its sequestered nature encourages the momentary exhilaration of love. Coverdale observes that the nature of their group "seemed to authorize any individual, of either sex, to fall in love with any other regardless of what would elsewhere be judged suitable and prudent" (III, 72). But such freedom is possible only because the community is at a great remove from the temporal, spatial, and ethical limitations of real life. Once Blithedale slips from its ideal and reflects more and more the considerations of the outside world, Coverdale sees unlimited love "mostly passing away with the state of things that had given it origin" (III, 72). Hence the novel offers in its conclusion an obverse reflection of the ending to *The House of the Seven Gables.* When Hollingworth's ego crumbles beneath the weight of Zenobia's accusations and he turns to Priscilla for support, the author once more has the chance to let love resolve the major tensions of the story and create an intentionally bright ending. But instead Hawthorne presents a qualified happiness, more in tune with the circumstances of life within the novel. Hollingsworth and his bride are not allowed to depart in happiness toward a rosy future. Instead, Zenobia warns Priscilla:

Poor child! Methinks you have but a melancholy lot before you, sitting all alone in that wide, cheerless heart, where, for aught you know—and as I, alas! believe—the fire which you have kindled may soon go out. Ah, the thought makes me shiver for you! What will you do, Priscilla, when you find no spark among the ashes? (III, 220)

Zenobia claims that for her part she will retreat to a nunnery, but in the end she does immeasurably more to darken the scene by committing suicide. Coverdale's realistic description of the dragging for her body and the resultant mutilation of her twisted corpse serve to conclude the action on a decidedly negative note.

Even after the action has come to a close, Coverdale cannot let Hollingsworth rest, but travels out for a follow-up story on the lovers. He finds that their happiness is limited by the memory of the tragedy at

Blithedale, and the novel concludes with the couple simply doing the best that they can. Coverdale then adds a moral about the dangers of philanthropy, with a timely reflection on Zenobia's body moldering in the earth. He argues that "It is because the spirit is inestimable, that the lifeless body is so little valued" (III, 244). There is no irresponsibly happy ending on earth, however. Hollingsworth has been reformed, but he must live out his life and find what happiness is possible within the conditions of life originally described by the novel. Hollingsworth is transformed, but not life itself.

The Marble Faun, like the other romances, contrasts moments of love with the demands of history. Its focus is the fawnlike Donatello, born into this world without the mark of Original Sin, who provides many idealistic moments for his group of friends. After a talk with Miriam, the sculptor Kenyon reflects on the transitory nature of such moments:

The fancy impressed him, that she, too, like Donatello, had reached a wayside Paradise, in their mysterious life-journey, where they both threw down the burthen of the Before and After, and, except for this interview with himself, were happy in the flitting moment. To-day, Donatello was the sylvan Faun; to-day, Miriam was his fit companion, a Nymph of grove or fountain; tomorrow—a remorseful Man and Woman, linked by a marriage-bond of crime—they would set forth towards an inevitable goal. (IV, 435)

Kenyon thus notices the strict temporal limitations of love's ideals within the context of the couple's personal history. But in *The Marble Faun* Hawthorne goes farther in evaluating these moments. They are not restricted to blissful love; any time in which emotion would cast away the demands of the past qualifies as an idealistic moment. When Donatello throws the model to his death, Miriam would have him "Forget it! Cast it all behind you!" Hawthorne observes that "guilt has its moments of rapture, too" and that "the foremost result of a broken law is ever an ecstatic sense of freedom" (IV, 176).

Idealistic moments, however, are not allowed to pass uncriticized. *The Marble Faun* is set in an artists' milieu, and the power of history is frequently discussed in aesthetic terms. Kenyon objects that "Flitting moments . . . ought not to be incrusted with the eternal repose of marble" (IV, 16), while Miriam later complements his theory by arguing for the expression of full existential context, that the Archangel Michael, pictured after his battle with Satan, should look like he has just battled the Devil (IV, 186). Rome, a city of art and history, is preeminently a place where one finds "everywhere . . . a Cross—and a nastiness at the foot of it" (IV, 111).

The ultimate complexity in *The Marble Faun* is no less than one of the most striking paradoxes in Christian theology: the Fortunate Fall. As applied to Donatello, this theme has received ample attention from Hawthorne scholars.[5] Its function in the resolution, however, centers on Kenyon and Hilda, and it is here that a helpful comparison with the other romances can be made. When Kenyon proposes this "perplexity" to Hilda, that sin may be ultimately good, she replies that such speculation is "terrible"; she accuses him of not perceiving "what a mockery your creed makes, not only of all religious sentiments, but of moral law, and how it annuls and obliterates whatever precepts of Heaven are written deepest within us" (IV, 460). She therefore refuses to consider the question. Some critics have suggested that Hawthorne is speaking through Hilda to express either his uncertainty about or distaste for this doctrine,[6] but in fact neither is Hilda fleeing reality nor is Hawthorne dodging the question. The point here made is certainly as valid as Herman Melville's in *Pierre:* that there are certain questions which human nature cannot trust itself to dwell upon. There is God's time and man's time, and while each is proper in its own sphere, the attempt to live absolutely by one time in the realm of the other leads inevitably to disaster. Man's fall is, of course, a certainty within Christian theology; Christ's subsequent redemption, again within this same doctrine, is an obvious good. There may exist a cause-and-effect relationship between the two which would make absolute, ideal sense; but in terms of the temporal context of earthly life such speculations could be destructive of faith, hope, and even sanity. The Fortunate Fall is a mystical, or suprarational, doctrine, and any attempt to translate it into earthly terms would in principle endorse the most horrible crimes in the name of the end justifying the means. Hawthorne's contemporary and close friend had shown in *Pierre* what happens when a person regulates his earthly chronometer by Heavenly Mean Time. Hawthorne shows the same awareness in the resolution to *The Marble Faun.* The lovers' ideal is not sufficient to transform historical necessity, but neither is historical necessity powerful enough to overthrow the ideal system of man's faith. In the ending to his last major romance Hawthorne counsels that reality and ideality do not mix, and that an attempted mixture welcomes chaos.

The resolutions of these romances suggest that love's idealistic moments do not endure, and that they become exceedingly suspect when placed in the context of history. Human life would be sterile without them, but one must realize, says Hawthorne, that man does not live his whole life at such emotional peaks. Especially foolish is the belief that subjective perceptions can erase, transform, or transcend one's historical context. Dimmesdale and Hester are wrong to suppose that their own good spirits will banish the social demands of the Puritan village; Miriam and Donatello are equally foolish to think that they can escape retribution for their crime of homicide. Positive thinking has its limits. In *The Blithedale Romance* the lovers do survive, but their happiness is moderated by the sad memory of Blithedale. Pure happiness remains beyond reach. Moreover, the resolutions of these romances refuse to endorse simple ideality or reality. Instead, real and ideal form a complex reflecting the deepest themes in Hawthorne's works: spiritual pride, lethal egotism, and the Fortunate Fall.

The House of the Seven Gables, however, was for Hawthorne a special problem. He had thought *The Scarlet Letter* "too sombre," finding it "impossible to relieve the shadow of the story with so much light as I would gladly have thrown in."[7] Whipple urged him to complete a novel "more relieved by touches of that beautiful and peculiar humor,"[8] as did his wife, who complained that even his own frontispiece portrait was too gloomy.[9] But the writing of *The House of the Seven Gables* became "a Slough of Despond."[10] On November 29, 1850, when he must have been nearly two-thirds through the manuscript, Hawthorne wrote his publisher that "I am weary and my hand trembles with writing all day at it." He revealed further, "It darkens damnably towards the close, but I shall try hard to pour some setting sunshine over it."[11] When Duyckinck's review appeared, emphasizing the gloominess, Hawthorne wrote him to complain that "I cannot quite understand why everything I write takes so melancholy an aspect in your eyes." He then admitted, "I suppose I was illuminated by my purpose to bring it to a prosperous close,"[12] but Duyckinck had been told this several months earlier by James T. Fields.[13] Whipple's essay, published in June, anticipated a century of criticism when he charged that the conclusion "departs from the integrity of the original conception, and interferes with the strict unity of the work."[14] Instead of challenging this view, Hawthorne finally admitted, "Whipple's notices have done more than pleased me, for they have helped me to see my book."[15]

The ending of *The House of the Seven Gables* should not, however, be viewed as a total anomaly within Hawthorne's work. He did "pour sunshine" over the concluding pages and allowed to a moment of love greater temporal and spatial powers than he did or would elsewhere. Yet his theme in this book was the inexorable demands of history, and the way he resolves the problem ironically emphasizes just how strong history is, for it takes nothing less than a transformation of the entire world to effect a satisfactory conclusion. Earlier Pyncheons had sought to end the curse by making restitution to the Maules. Gervayse Pyncheon, however, was halted by the spectre of the old Colonel himself, while the elder Jaffrey was dissuaded by "the strong prejudice of propinquity," which "In all the Pyncheons . . . had the energy of disease" (II, 23). Love is the only effective resolution. Whether Hawthorne presents the act as high irony or sincere belief, the product is the same: Holgrave and Phoebe must "transfigure the Earth and make it Eden again" to resolve problems which in the historical frame defy resolution.

In his later career Hawthorne labored over four abortive romances, each concerned with an elixir of life. Hester and Dimmesdale found no effective elixir at the brookside; nor could Miriam and Donatello retreat to a prelapsarian innocence. As with the old folks of "Dr. Heidegger's Experiment," Hawthorne's characters typically fail in such a search. History remains inexorable. Hollingsworth and Priscilla find only a diminished bliss, while Fanshawe despairs of any; the lovers of *The Scarlet Letter* and *The Marble Faun* anticipate happiness only in an afterlife. The ending to *The House of the Seven Gables* is Hawthorne's experiment in sustaining the New Jerusalem on earth and granting subjective idealism any effective power over the realities of the historical situation. Yet it demonstrates the same thesis as his other romances, only in an obverse manner. Hawthorne was dissatisfied with the gloom of his other works, but he did not have to alter his basic statement in order to infuse "setting sunshine." Although the ending fails in form, its thematic content remains one with the endings to the other major romances.

Ethic and Aesthetic: Basil and Isabel
March Stories of William Dean Howells

BASIL AND ISABEL MARCH were the characters used by William Dean Howells both in his first and much later experiments with novelistic art. Because their early adventures so closely parallel Howells' own, they are usually discussed as the fictional counterparts of William Dean and Elinor Howells.[1] Most studies of the minor novels in which they appear center on the biographical clues they offer toward an understanding of Howells' approach to realism.[2] Yet it is Howells' major biographer, Edwin H. Cady, who most vehemently objects to such criticism:

But the bridal couple of *Their Wedding Journey,* Basil and Isabel March, are not Will and Elinor Howells. They are products of Howells' imagination just as Hamlet was the product of Shakespeare's. . . . Both were trying, and each in his own way succeeded, to create a structure of illusions which would make the words they placed upon the page stir the imagination of the reader. Both were forced to rely on their power to stir the imagination through illusion and so to entice or command that imagination to create experience within the reader's mind.[3]

Because of their role in his evolving literary imagination, there is a unified theme to the March narratives which deserves treatment for its own richness of development and for the elaborate parallel it offers not simply to Howells' early biographical notebook approach to literary realism, but rather to his deepest experience as a creatively imaginative artist. There exists in the March stories a theme that begins in *Their Wedding Journey,* makes a major statement in *A Hazard of New Fortunes,* and finds more depth and complexity in the minor works of the 1890s. The theme is progressively expressed by the style in which Basil

Reprinted by permission from *Modern Fiction Studies,* copyright 1970 by Purdue Research Foundation, West Lafayette, Indiana, U.S.A.

and Isabel March discover the proper way to view America in the 1870s, the way they come to an understanding of the urban crisis of the 1890s, and the manner in which they face the responsibility of personal moral acts in their later dealings. Each step is marked by the couple's fondness for the aesthetic point of view and their eventual subordination of it to a more ethical perspective. The Marches' need for the aesthetic is reflected in their habit of romantically sentimentalizing all they see, as they turn to fantasy and fabulation of persons, places, and things in order to satisfy their immense curiosity and desire for vicarious adventure. Each successive adventure, however, returns the couple to the brink of ethical perspective, allowing Howells a context for moral statement within his evolving fictional form. In their yearning for the picturesque rather than the actual the Marches indeed reflect Howells' early ambivalence between the romantic and the real, as previous studies have shown. But it is attention to the aesthetic-ethic on a thematic level that shows the Marches and their behavior most fully as the products of Howells' literary imagination and presents an analogy to the author's own problems with the responsibility of the creative artist.

Howells begins *Their Wedding Journey* with a narrative disclaimer which some would read only as a manifesto for a new realism, but which more specifically indicates his plans for the Marches and their role in this novel: "I shall have nothing to do," confides Howells, "but to talk of some ordinary traits of American life *as these appeared to them*" (italics added).[4] The emphasis is just, for the virtues and limitations of their perceptions constitute the major rhythm of the action, the play between the aesthetic and the ethic. This first novel followed two successful travel books, *Venetian Life* and *Italian Journeys,* that had profited from Howells' own casual manner of personal description. *Their Wedding Journey* would test this same method for fiction.

The aesthetic-ethic split is stressed in the first incident of their journey, the hailstorm which forces them to change their mode of travel. Although the storm is causing suffering, rather discreetly to them and more seriously to others, Basil and Isabel accept it as aesthetic. They are aware of the dangerously crowded streetcar and the "horses that pranced and leaped under the stinging blows of the hail-stones," but ultimately "our friends felt as if it were an effective and very naturalistic bit of pantomime contrived for their admiration." Indeed, "There was something theatrical about it all" (p. 4). As the Marches commence their journey, they often turn to the aesthetic as a measure taken against boredom, and, as food for their curiosity, romanticize nearly everything in sight. They are fully aware of what they are doing, and such knowledge adds to their own enjoyment, as well as to the complexity of the problem, as they secure themselves against the waiting-room boredom by fabulating from the materials at hand. We learn that "In the course of their observations they formed many cordial friendships and bitter enmities upon the ground of personal appearance, or particulars of dress, with people whom they saw for a half a minute upon an average" (p. 11). They become delightfully caught up in their daydreaming, until their feeling for one passing character becomes so strong that "if they had been friends of the young man and his family for generations, and felt bound if any harm befell him to go and break the news gently to his parents, their nerves could not have been more intimately wrought upon by his hazardous behavior" (pp. 11–12). But such vicarious toying with the ethical is merely sentimental, and "after all was said and thought, it was only eight o'clock, and they still had an hour to wait." (p. 12).

The Marches need the panorama of other people to complete their aesthetic appreciation of the scenes they meet on their journey; putting persons in his pictures had been part of Howells' descriptive technique in his travel books before. Facing New York's Broadway, Basil answers Isabel's disappointment with the statement, "Perhaps the street has some possible grandeur of its own, though it needs a multitude of people to bring out its best effect." What turns the trick are "those human rapids," whose "Niagara roar" is "always like a strong wine" to him (p. 28). But when people fail to answer the aesthetic call and become more real than romantic, Isabel pouts. The noble, intriguing foreigner on the St. Lawrence boat becomes, upon investigation, a fifty-fourth degree Odd Fellow with a disgusting New York accent, and the Indians of Niagara Falls horrify Isabel with their "distressingly good English," silk hats, Protestant religion, and general good health (p. 138).

To this point the Marches' aestheticizing has seemed innocent enough, but as they come upon forms of actual suffering which would demand an ethical response, they cannot help but treat them as aesthetic. In Montreal the newlyweds are happily reminded of "the enviably deplorable countries we all love" (p. 201) where one can be so fortunate as to come upon "the glorious likeness of an Italian beggar" (p. 202) and other pleasurable grotesques. Such passages could be troublesome were it not clear from the start that Howells is intending satire of his blithesome couple. In New York City touring the streets he has caught the young bride poised between the two elements of aesthetic and ethic: " 'How lovely!' said Isabel, swiftly catching at her skirt, and deftly escaping contact with one of a long row of ash-barrels posted sentinel-like on the edge of the pavement" (p. 23). To make it perfectly clear, Howells reminds us that these were the ash barrels "in which the decrepit children and mothers of the streets were clawing for bits of coal" (p. 26).

Yet what is most striking about the Marches' behavior is that several times they come close to a real ethic, but once again retreat into the aesthetic. Driving through the city streets, they are impressed by the "endless blocks of brownstone fronts," and have enough sensibility so that the view "oppressed them like a procession of houses trying to pass a given point and never getting by." But when it comes to the people inside those houses, the best the Marches can do is fantasize "that the daily New York murder might even at that moment be somewhere taking place":

. . . they morbidly wondered what the day's murder would be, and in what swarming tenement-house, or den of the assassin streets by the river-sides,—if indeed it did not befall in some such high, close-shuttered, handsome dwellings as those they passed, in whose twilight it would be so easy to strike down the master and leave him undiscovered and unmourned by the family ignorantly absent at the mountain or the sea side. They conjectured of the horror of midsummer battles, and pictured the anguish of ship-wrecked men upon a tropical coast, and the grimy misery of stevedores unloading shiny cargoes of anthracite coal at city docks. But now at last, as they took seats opposite one another in the crowded car, they seemed to have drifted infinite distances and long epochs asunder. They looked hopelessly across the intervening gulf, and mutely questioned when it was and from what far city they or some remote ancestors of theirs had set forth upon a wedding journey. They bade each other a tacit farewell, and with patient, pathetic faces awaited the end of the world. (p. 48)

What began as an ethical interest has become a purely aesthetic dream that can hardly be stopped; indeed, this quality of the imaginary journey anticipates, on a whimsical level, Mark Twain's more serious voyage of "The Great Dark," where a flight of fancy becomes so long and complex that the characters also conclude looking hopelessly across the gulf between reality and fantasy, unsure even of when the trip began.

Although the Marches' unbridled imagination, as opposed to the Edwards' in Twain's story, is harmlessly comic, at times one believes that it is hard for the Marches to feel humane at all, as Howells indicates when he describes the night-boat accident. "Why, I only heard a very slight tinkling of the chandeliers," a lady says. "Is it such a very slight matter to run down another boat and sink it?" (p. 73). For the disinterested spectator it can be, and although Howells notes that "a burden was carried from which fluttered, with its terrible regularity, that utterance of mortal anguish," one is impressed that what Basil hears is "a hollow, moaning, gurgling sound, regular as that of the machinery, for some note of which he mistook it." And the next morning a river comrade can appear "in the picturesque immortal attitudes of Raphael's Galilean fisherman," while Basil is "thinking with a certain luxurious compassion of the scalded man." "This poor wretch," we are told, "seemed of another order of beings, as the calamitous always seem to the happy, and Basil's pity was quite an abstraction; which, again, amused and shocked him" (pp. 77–78).

The Marches together at one point do reflect on the very problem of acting humanely, after they have witnessed a man's collapse from sunstroke. Basil has at first treated the matter aesthetically, and Howells as narrator is merciless: "Basil drank his soda and paused to look upon this group, which he felt would commend itself to realistic sculpture as eminently characteristic of the local life, and as 'The Sunstroke' would sell enormously in the hot season" (p. 51). Isabel, though, is horrified by the scene, upset that it might have been Basil. "If anything did happen to you in New York," she complains, "I should like to have the spectators look as if they saw a human being in trouble." Basil defends himself and the other bystanders with an answer that aptly describes the Marches' own position in relation to the events of their journey:

"Nothing is so hard as to understand that there are human beings in this world besides one's self and one's set. But let us be selfishly thankful that it isn't you and I there in the apothecary's shop, as it might very well be; and let us get to the boat as soon as we can, and end this horrible midsummer-day's dream. We must have a carriage," he added with tardy wisdom, hailing an empty hack, "as we ought to have had all day; though I'm not sorry, now the worst's over, to have seen the worst." (pp. 54–55)

The imaginary voyage, Howells is telling us, does have its terrors, once one yields his romantic security and grapples with ethical facts. In their mutually self-centered love the couple are protected, and it is from this position that they safely romanticize. To make their journey interesting with the least expense of spirit, it would seem, the Marches cultivate the aesthetic. When they fail at last "to extract any sentiment from the scene without," they promptly turn "their faces from the window," and look "about them for amusement within the car" (p. 86). They are "tourists" who "comfortably sentimentalized the scene behind the close-drawn curtains of their carriage" (p. 239); provincial in time as well as space, they view the awesomeness of history from a sequestered position that grants full license to the aesthetic: "He and Isabel enjoyed the lurid picture with all the zest of sentimentalists dwelling upon the troubles of other times from the shelter of the safe and peaceful present. They were

23

both poets in their quality of bridal couple, and so long as their own nerves were unshaken they could transmute all facts to entertaining fables" (p. 143). And they are rarely shaken because, despite the scenes they view in Canada and even America, they have "the patronizing spirit of travellers in a foreign country" (p. 12). Prejudiced by their European experiences, the Marches "could not think of anyone's loving New York as Dante loved Florence, or as Madame de Staël loved Paris, or as Johnson loved black, homely, home-like London" (p. 33). Olov Fryckstedt has noted that "It was a part of Howells' slow discovery of the nature of America that he should . . . discard the search for the picturesque as an artistic approach,"[5] and it is not surprising to find him calling his characters to task for viewing America the way they falsely perceived Europe.

But the picturesque habit, strong as it is, is only half of the Marches' limitations. In "the immense complex drama" about them "they were both actors and spectators" (p. 70), but the solipsism of their love removes them, on this first journey, from much of the action. "They . . . were in it but not of it" (p. 50), and might not truly be until the experience of *A Hazard of New Fortunes* would teach Basil the fact of the complicity of all men in each others' affairs. For now, "All the loveliness that exists out of you," Basil tells Isabel, "is mere pageant to me" (p. 64). We imagine the feeling is mutual, and hence such irresponsible fabulating as her compulsion to fall down in confession "to any one of the black-robed priests upon the street" (p. 196) is explained by her final dream that "She was confessing to the priest, and she was not at all surprised to find that he was Basil in a suit of mediaeval armor" (p. 227). All her fantasies ultimately center on him, for he is the center of her love.

Much of the journey takes this as its theme: secure within their love, the Marches enjoy the aesthetic entertainment of their wedding trip, a virtual travelogue in motion. But the last incident on the tour becomes the climax which indicates a growth beyond the aesthetic that will be developed in *A Hazard of New Fortunes*. Upon checking into their Quebec hotel, the Marches and the Ellisons (whom they have met and joined at Niagara) find that their customary suites are not available; only two rooms are left, so the men double up, allowing Isabel, Kitty, and Mrs. Ellison to share the remaining facility. Such discomfort is not the least indignity, however, for Basil and Colonel Ellison find a young lady in their room, one of a troupe of strolling players who occupy that whole floor; the confusion is eventually remedied, but only after several inconveniencing interruptions. Finally, having accepted without blush the ultimate insult of mismatched tablecloth sheets, Basil and the Colonel retire to sleep. Almost at once Basil is awakened: the actors have taken over the courtyard to serenade a fellow and the ensuing racket promises a sleep-less night, but the beleaguered bridegroom trusts his aesthetic to see him through:

All this, abstractly speaking, was nothing to Basil; yet he could recollect few things intended for his pleasure that had given him more satisfaction. He thought, as he glanced out into the moonlight on the high-gabled silvery roofs around and on the gardens of the convents and the towers of the quaint city, that the scene wanted nothing of the proper charm of Spanish humor and romance, and he was as grateful to those poor souls as if they had meant him a favor. (p. 276)

This is the typical March aesthetic, and the incident seems to be drawing it all together, as the troupe's "love-making was the last touch of a com-edy that Basil could hardly accept as reality, it was so much more like something seen upon the stage" (p. 227). But, as he falls back into sleep, we see evidence of a major change on Basil's part, for instead of follow-ing his and Isabel's customary pattern of working from ethic to aesthetic, he now follows from the aesthetic to the ethic: "he was conscious of one subtle touch of compassion for those poor strollers,—a pity so delicate and fine and tender that it hardly seemed his own but rather a sense of the compassion that pities the whole world" (p. 227). But if this would seem to be the fine ending to the aesthetic-ethic imbalance that has char-acterized so much of the wedding journey, we must look again. As he will do later in *A Hazard of New Fortunes,* Howells is careful to not overly romanticize his own novel with a sentimental conclusion. Basil March has indeed experienced a moral growth, tenuous though it is (compassion for the players' troupe is weakly suggestive of the Ancient Mariner's blessing of the water snakes), yet Howells keeps the event in its true perspective.

Basil returns to Boston exhilarated by the journey and, we suppose, by his new moral posture. He proves the latter by his warmth and candor with "a man for whom he ordinarily cared nothing, and whom he would perhaps rather have gone out . . . to avoid than have spoken to; but now he plunged at him with effusion, and wrung his hand, smiling from ear to ear." A magnificent scene of brotherly love, and the dawn of a bosom friendship? Howells strikes dead the romantic impulse: "The other re-mained coldly unaffected, after a first start of surprise at his cordiality, and then reviled the dust and heat. 'But I'm going to take a little run down to Newport, to-morrow, for a week,' he said. 'By the way, you look as if *you* needed a little change. Aren't you going anywhere this summer?" (p. 286) "So you see, my dear," Basil confesses to Isabel,

25

"our travels are incommunicably our own. . . . Even if we tried, we couldn't make our wedding-journey theirs" (pp. 286–87). The moral growth, too, is incommunicably their own; it is indeed ironic that, after remaining inhumanely isolated within their own selfish aesthetic, their element of ethical "involvement" should also be a very personal possession. But Howells will make the same arrangement at the end of *A Hazard of New Fortunes* also. After a long period of ethical education Basil will appreciate the doctrine of complicity, but still will be disallowed any romantically spectacular action. The Marches, at the end of *A Hazard of New Fortunes,* remain essentially within their own selves and principles, as they do here at the end of *Their Wedding Journey;* it is the growth from what they have been in themselves that is important.

The progress of Basil March toward an understanding of the theory of "complicity" has been well documented,[6] and constitutes the accepted reading of *A Hazard of New Fortunes.*[7] But attention should be given to the aesthetic-ethic imbalance that precedes it, for here are to be found many striking similarities to *Their Wedding Journey* and to the works that follow.

As we meet the Marches, nearly twenty years later, we find that they still delight in aesthetic adventures, as "They liked to play with the romantic, from the safe vantage-ground of their real practicality, and to divine the poetry of the commonplace" (I, 26). As they take their new journey, this time a permanent move to New York City, the old aesthetic habit seems innocent enough; at times it offers opportunities for real beauty, as when their appreciation of the elevated railway at night allows Howells one of his more striking passages of description:

The track that found and lost itself a thousand times in the flare and tremor of the innumerable lights; the moony sheen of electrics mixing with the reddish points and blots of gas far and near; the architectural shapes of houses and churches and towers, rescued by the obscurity from all that was ignoble in them, and the coming and going of the trains marking the stations with vivider or fainter plumes of flameshot steam—formed an incomparable perspective. (I, 95–96)

The situation is the more interesting, however, because of the unique opportunity that travel along the El offers. To Basil, "it was better than the theatre, of which it reminded him, to see those people through their windows." Here indeed are the curious couple of *Their Wedding Journey,* as they exclaim, "What suggestion! what drama! what infinite interest" (I, 95).

"To play with the romantic . . . to divine the poetry of the commonplace." As they are introduced to the city through their house-hunting forays, the Marches do much of this. But they find only poetry in the commonplace, and never suffering. In Washington Square "They met the familiar picturesque raggedness of southern Europe with the old kindly illusion that somehow it existed for their appreciation and that it found adequate compensation for poverty in this," and March considers his ethical debt paid in full by "letting a little Neopolitan put a superfluous shine on his boots" (I, 67). Enthralled with the picturesque, they prefer Mott Street to Fifth Avenue, and Isabel, having added an infatuation with a "colored janitor" to her romance with the black waiter of *Their Wedding Journey,* now declares, "It's true. I *am* in love with the whole race," primarily because "they" are so "angelic" (I, 57). As for the suffering of any group in the city, Isabel confidently announces that there is none: "that is, it would be suffering from our point of view, but they've been used to it all their lives, and they don't feel discomfort so much" (I, 86). For the Marches' sake one hopes the poor do not, as Basil allows that even if there is suffering, "they're so gay about it all" (I, 76).

Also, as in *Their Wedding Journey,* the roots of their aestheticism can be traced to their initial motivation for their travels. In the earlier novel the Marches sought the picturesque to rival their European experience; now again, from a greater distance in time, they wish "to gratify an aesthetic sense, to renew the faded pleasure of travel for a moment, to get back into the Europe of our youth" (I, 66). To complicate the endeavor, America itself has "faded," and as "They recalled the Broadway of five, of ten, of twenty years ago, swelling and roaring with a tide of gaily painted omnibuses and of picturesque traffic," they miss "the tumultuous perspective of former times" (I, 65). The aestheticizing must serve a double purpose, not just imparting to America the European picturesque, but restoring to the 1890s the charm and fancy of their wedding journey of the 1870s.

Such a task, of course, is impossible. The Marches are inescapably twenty years older, and the country itself has changed, as suits Howells' purpose in writing this novel. The social crisis to which Howells awakened at this time has been well described,[8] and the Marches' position is in fact the making of the novel. "We're imprisoned in the present" (I, 73), says Basil, a present which in its realities belies the fanciful aesthetic that he and his wife try to impose upon it. In their move to New York they have tried desperately to organize the prospect of the city into a romantic picture, and despite all setbacks are resolved to remain happy. "It's the unhappy who see unhappiness" (I, 89), March observes in another context, but the implication fits himself as well. To see the social reality of New York in ethical terms, he and Isabel must undergo a change.

While the Marches maintain their equilibrium, there is little chance to pierce to the ethical center, to the humanity resident in the scenes they observe. Basil rides the streetcars in search of "some interesting shape of shabby adversity" (I, 242), but Howells reveals,

It must be owned that he did not take much trouble about this; what these poor people were thinking, hoping, fearing, enjoying, suffering; just where and how they lived; who and what they indvidually were—these were the matters of his waking dreams as he stared hard at them, while the train raced further into the gray ugliness—the shapeless, graceless, reckless picturesqueness of the Bowery. (I, 243)

But because he is lax to consciously attend the ethical, Basil finds it hard to act on any level but the aesthetic. Even when an ethical response beckons, as when his interest in a group of disembarking immigrants leads him to wish that for their welfare the government would "follow each of them to his home, wherever he meant to fix it within our borders," the ethic becomes at once aesthetic, and we learn that "he intended to work them up into a dramatic effect in some sketch"; the result is that "they remained mere material in his memorandum-book, together with some quaint old houses on the Sixth Avenue road" (II, 72). In an earlier piece of banter concerning the slums, Basil had chided Isabel that "we must change the conditions"; Isabel replied, "Oh no; we must go to the theatre and forget them" (I, 88). By continually regarding the social conditions of the city as food for his aesthetic sensibility and as material for his sketchbook, Basil is effectively "going to the theatre and forgetting them" too.

It is imperative to note that Howells as narrator is fully aware of the ethical implications of the scenes visited by his characters. On one of their house hunts the Marches come upon what Howells describes[9] as an "abode of the extremest poverty," most particularly "a poverty as hopeless as any in the world, transmitting itself from generation to generation, and establishing conditions of permanency to which human life adjusts itself as it does to those of some incurable disease, like leprosy." "The time had been," we are told, "when the Marches would have taken a purely aesthetic view of the facts as they glimpsed them in this street of tenement-houses," and judging it "as picturesque as a street in Naples or Florence" have wondered "why nobody came to paint it" (I, 80). Their reaction even now, though, is not so different, as Isabel urges her husband to "work some of these New York sights up for *Every Other Week,*" the literary-aesthetic equivalent to a street painting. Most damning is Basil's reaction, that "the children of discomfort cheered him" (I, 81–82), even though he chides Isabel (to no avail) about the irony of their demands in the face of such poverty, for a "suitable" house. The best March can do is reflect that these tenements have more "family sweetness" (I, 84) than the pretentious marble-halled flats they have been inspecting.

Although Basil's street sketches fail to teach him the moral problems at hand, his economic association with the magazine that prints them eventually does. The way he must be educated is not to spend any amount of time sightseeing in the slums, but rather to have an alien economic power over his own life, as the lives of the tenement dwellers are so determined. The mere figure of Dryfoos the tycoon has struck March's ethic: whereas Fulkerson remains interested in the combination of his "picturesque past" and his "aesthetic present" (II, 44), March is more taken with the man's inevitable "moral deteriorization" (I, 297), and regrets that "such a man and his experience are the ideal and ambition of most Americans. I rather think they came pretty near being mine, once" (I, 297). Working with and indeed being controlled by such a man, Basil learns his lesson in social economics, and the mystery of the city unfolds to him and his wife:

> Their point of view was singularly unchanged, and their impressions of New York remained the same that they had been fifteen years before: huge, noisy ugly, kindly, it seemed to them now as it seemed then. *The main difference was that they saw it more now as a life, and then only regarded it a spectacle;* and March could not release himself from a sense of complicity with it, no matter what whimsical, or alien, or critical, attitude he took. A sense of the striving and the suffering deeply possessed him; and *this grew the more intense as he gained some knowledge of the forces at work.* . . . She lamented the literary peace, the intellectual refinement of the life they had left behind them; and he owned it was very pretty, but he said it was not life—it was death-in-life. [italics added] (II, 74)

Here is their recognition of the vitality of the ethical, and the lifelessness of the purely aesthetic interest in life.

One might expect, were this a novel of purely economic protest, that the Marches would gallantly challenge the order and perhaps break the system. Basil resolves to resign in protest against Dryfoos' tyranny and become a freelance writer in order to fight "in whatever cause he thought just," with "no ties, no chains" (II, 145), but before they can even complete their daydream the word arrives that Dryfoos has relented. There is no chance now for such action, and "They felt themselves slipping down from the moral height which they had gained" (II, 147), leaving the Marches with only their new ethical sensibility and its concomitant principles of life. Does this deflate the Marches' achievement and upset the novel's structure, which has been so patiently leading to just such a moral victory? Not at all, says George Arms, unless we would want from Howells a sentimental, rather than a realistic, novel.[10] Basil March's response, on an ethical rather than on an active economic level, indicates Howells' own thoughts on the situation. Robert L. Hough has shown that Howells' criticism of capitalism in society, although taking its cue from the economic idiom, "was almost wholly moral and humanistic. It was not basically economic."[11] It is communication on the most basic human level that is impossible in an economic caste society, a theme which Hough sees Howells treat "many times in his novels—in *Annie Kilburn, The Minister's Charge, A Hazard of New Fortunes,* and *A Traveler from Altruria.* "[12] Hence to have March become a crusader for a new economics would not only have made him, as Arms would say, a romanticized hero, but would displace *A Hazard of New Fortunes* from the center of Howells' own social theory.

A Hazard of New Fortunes brings the Marches to the climax of their growth from the aesthetic to the ethic. With Basil's realization that his fortunes are complicit with those of other men, he marks his greatest distance from the notion that other persons, places, and things exist for his and Isabel's fanciful entertainment. George C. Carrington, Jr., has called *Their Wedding Journey* "Howells' *Mardi,* a voyage in search of perception and meaning."[13] Although we have seen that the conclusion to this first journey indicates progress toward an ethical view of life, the experiences twenty years later bring that moral growth to a fuller fruition.

Between the writing of *Their Wedding Journey* and *A Hazard of New Fortunes* Howells offered only two narratives in which the Marches figure: *A Chance Acquaintance,* where they function peripherally as friends of Miss Kitty Ellison, and the brief *Niagara Revisited, Twelve Years after Their Wedding Journey.* But after *A Hazard of New Fortunes* Howells published two each of short novels, long stories, and travel books in which Basil and Isabel March are prominently featured. The novels and stories, all narrated in the first person by Basil himself,[14] appeared between 1890 and 1897. These four narratives deal explicitly with the ethic-aesthetic problem, and mark an advance over the achievement of *A Hazard of New Fortunes* in both the Marches' own posture and in Howells' artistic use of the theme.

One advance that the Marches have made is that they are more cautious about intruding into other people's affairs. In the first adventure, the short novel *The Shadow of a Dream,* Basil is proud that, for the most part, he and Isabel have "kept about our own business" (p. 102), and as soon as he sees "that it was not my affair . . . I decided not to put my fingers between the bark and the tree" (p. 122).[15] In the two stories "A Pair of Patient Lovers" and "A Circle in the Water" the Marches regret in the first instance being exposed to "this abnormal situation" (p. 36) and in the second "did not want to have anything to do" with it at all (p. 294).[16] Such disclaimers recur constantly in these narratives.

A second advance is that instead of only aestheticizing the situation they must face, the Marches become, albeit reluctantly, ethical advisors to the moral dilemmas that people present them. *The Shadow of a Dream,* in fact, allows Basil March to handle a problem resulting from a pathological confusion of the aesthetic with the ethic. The victim has been Douglas Faulkner, whose romantic inclinations have caused him to fancy his recurrent nightmare as indicative of a deeper moral disease. Basil argues that this is nonsense, that it is superstitious to find ethical significance in one's dreams. Faulkner, however, succumbs to his mania and bequeaths a second moral dilemma for Basil to solve. The fancy has been that Faulkner's wife has been in love with the friend and houseguest Rev. James Nevil, and now that Faulkner has died, Nevil dare not consummate his subsequent love for Hermia Faulkner due to his own fear that he may have unintentionally harbored adulterous thoughts while Faulkner was alive. This is the moral scruple which, in *A Modern Instance,* keeps Ben Halleck from marrying Bartley Hubbard's widow. Now, eight years later, Howells takes the opportunity, through the character of Basil March, to condemn this scruple of a similar clergyman. "What mere madness of the moon," groans Basil, for Nevil's behavior is that of a "moral hypochondriac" (p. 209). In "A Pair of Patient Lovers" Basil must advise still another clergyman with a similar problem, this time the Reverend Arthur Glendenning, who has submitted to the comparatively artificial dilemma of becoming engaged to a girl whose mother will then not allow them to marry. Glendenning is totally distraught by what Basil can see is a "position which isn't at all uncommon with engaged people, of having to wait upon exterior circumstances before you get married" (pp. 41–42). Basil tells the minister "that no moral scruple presented itself to him," and that "when it came to the point, he was simply and naturally a lover, like any other man" (p. 45).

But along with the greater ethical perspective comes the aesthetic tendency the Marches have yet to escape. Even in the very moral *The Shadow of a Dream* Basil finds that he must acknowledge "a good deal of curiosity as well as some humanity," and duly feels ashamed of his motives when he first goes to meet the ailing Faulkner (p. 16). Isabel promptly "romances" Hermia, beginning their typical set piece which invites Basil to "romance poor old Faulkner" (p. 37). At the conclusion of the story the Marches' sincere concern for their friends is mixed with a wish to fictionalize a more aesthetically pleasing ending to their experience: "My wife and I have often talked of [Hermia] and Nevil, and have tried to see some way for them out of the shadow of Faulkner's dream into a sunny and happy life. As they are both dead, we have dealt with them as arbitrarily as with the personages in a fiction, and have placed and replaced them at our pleasure in the game, which they played so disastrously, so that we could bring it to a fortunate close for them" (pp. 215–16). But even Basil is unhappy with his fantasy, finding it "too like what I have found carried out in some very romantic novels" (p. 217). In "A Pair of Patient Lovers," moreover, Isabel's fancy for the two young people becomes so dominant that it is "as if she had invented them and set them going in their advance toward each other, like two mechanical toys" (p. 12). Basil himself likes to imagine for them a course of life that would be "rather Hawthornesque" (p. 53), and his ultimate fancy, of Edith literally dying of joy when her mother yields to her marriage, is too "tawdry" a romanticization for even Isabel (p. 74).

It would be a mistake, however, to charge the Marches with the same debility they suffered from in *Their Wedding Journey,* and to fault Howells for making no more of the aesthetic-ethic theme than he did then. Much more is done with that theme, largely because of the possibilities offered by the Marches' improved stature. Although Howells wrote these four narratives after *A Hazard of New Fortunes,* only the events of *An Open-Eyed Conspiracy* take place historically after the New York City experience. But we can see in Howells' own experiments with the aesthetic-ethic theme that he was progressing according to his own chronology toward more richness and complexity with the subject. *Their Wedding Journey* and *A Hazard of New Fortunes* present an aesthetic-ethic conflict in simple terms; the Marches mature, by means of an education to the realities of life and humanity, from the aesthetic to the ethic. In the narratives written after 1890, however, the Marches become more capable in the field of ethics; indeed, Basil becomes adept at moral counseling, trying to square the affairs of two clergymen who should themselves have known better. And with the publication of "A Circle in the Water" and *An Open-Eyed Conspiracy* we see the Marches' adventures take on an added dimension, that of their own creative responsibility for what their aesthetic fancies have set in motion.

"A Circle in the Water" concerns the Marches' interest in the filial bond between the ex-convict Tedham and his daughter Fay. Basil turns to the aesthetic as he ponders the problem:

"Now, how unhandsome life is!" I broke out, at one point on our way home, after we had turned the affair over in every light, and then dropped it, and then taken it up again. *"It's so graceless, so tasteless!* Why didn't Tedham die before the expiration of his term and solve all this knotty problem with dignity? Why should he have lived on this shabby way and come out and wished to see his daughter? *If there had been anything dramatic, anything artistic in the man's nature,* he would have renounced the claim his mere paternity gives him on her love, and left word with me that he had gone away and would never be heard of any more. That was the least he could have done." [italics added] (p. 341)

And that, after the Marches suggest that he not intrude upon the innocent girl, is exactly what he does do. Basil feels "a strange pleasure" from "the poignancy of a despair" not his own (p. 342), and he has effected in reality his aestheticized notion of how the affair should conclude. Isabel, however, becomes horrified that he has actually prompted such action, and holds him "responsible for the dilemma [he] had conjectured" and culpable "for that which had really presented itself" (p. 343). Fay, it turns out, strongly desires to see her father, and the Marches suffer for their aesthetic interference:

We had not been willing to let God alone, or to trust his leading; we had thought to improve on his management of the case, and to invent a principle for poor Tedham that should be better for him to act upon than the love of his child, which God had put into the man's heart, and which was probably the best thing that had ever been there. Well, we got our come-uppings, as the country people say, and however we might reason it away we had made ourselves responsible for the event. (pp. 355–56)

Howells has returned the Marches to their aesthetic fabulating in order to strike a new note on the earlier theme, as Basil and Isabel's achievement becomes more than a simple growth from aesthetic to ethic; for the first time they consciously face the awful responsibility of imaginative creativity.

An Open-Eyed Conspiracy, both written and historically set after the events of *A Hazard of New Fortunes,* is the test of Howells' greater theme.[17] The action takes place not in the potentially moralistic setting of urban slums but rather at the Saratoga resorts, and concerns not the weighty matter of an ex-convict reclaiming his estranged daughter, but instead the apparently frivolous occasion of a matchmaking. The Marches enjoy their vacation by resorting to what seems to be the manner of *Their Wedding Journey* over twenty years before, and Basil can boast "that we do not miss a single balloon ascension or pyrotechnic display" (p. 7). Nor does he miss the picturesque possibilities of the beautiful Cuban women, the scene of a French-Canadian mother chastising her little boy, or the presence of a dejected young girl. To the latter event he sits eavesdropping with all his might, and when she is joined by friends he resolves upon "aesthetically shadowing them" (p. 14). The girl is bored with her vacation, Basil surmises, and he confides to the reader that "I was poignantly interested in the little situation I had created" (p. 11). He hurries to tell Isabel of his "very rare and thrilling adventure"; she, however, proclaims it one of his interminable "romances about young girls being off and disappointed of a good time" (p. 19). His aesthetic is more refined, however, for he believes that he "can ultimately get some literature out of them," and cautions his wife, "I simply used these people conjecturally to give myself an agreeable pang. I didn't want to know anything more about them than I imagined, and I certainly didn't dream of doing anything for them. You'll spoil everything if you turn them from fiction into fact, and try to manipulate their destiny. Let them alone; they will work it out for themselves " (p. 40). If there is to be a moral drama, it will be within Basil's aesthetic imagination. But almost immediately he and Isabel interfere. When his young associate Kendricks shows up at the resort, himself looking for magazine copy, Basil offers him "just the heroine" for his Saratoga story (p. 74), and incidentally draws the young bachelor into his own fabulation. Continuing with his aesthetic plotting, March half-intentionally sneaks after them in a fog in order to be privy to their intimacies, and turns over in his mind "the several accidents which are employed in novels to bring young people to a realizing sense of their feelings toward each other" and wonders "which of them [he] might most safely invoke" (p. 127). At one point the distinction between fact and fiction becomes so blurred that we find Basil fictionalizing Julia's dance card in order to make her courtship fulfill more perfectly Isabel's idea of what it should be.

Soon Isabel becomes horrified at what she and Basil have done. The love affair that they started as their own aesthetic adventure has become on Julia's part a reality, and the older woman feels the awful responsibility for it. "Such a girl," she tells her husband, "couldn't imagine that we had simply got Mr. Kendricks to go about with her from a romantic wish to make her have a good time, and that he was doing it to oblige us, and wasn't at all interested in her" (p. 121). Basil sees that "I was the cause of all this trouble, and that if it had not been for me there would have been, as far as Mrs. March was concerned, no Miss Gage, and no love-affair of hers to deal with" (p. 148). He confesses to Kendricks "the responsibility which Mrs. March and myself had incurred by letting our sympathy for her run away with us" (p. 155), but to him the Marches fail to appear "the trembling arbiters of her destiny" as they feel themselves to be (p. 156). All does turn out well, but only after the Marches learn a sense of responsibility for their aesthetic creation. As the affair draws to a close Basil is tempted to act for Julia in regard to her opposed father, but he wisely "turns away" in order to let her own will effect the happy conclusion.

An Open-Eyed Conspiracy, in comparison to the weighty subjects of *A Hazard of New Fortunes* and "A Circle in the Water,' may not seem as serious. The character Basil March would himself appear to realize this, as he begs appreciation for the "anxieties which had been none the less real and constant because so often burlesqued" (p. 161). But we must consider the uses that Howells had made of the aesthetic-ethic theme in order to appreciate his achievement in this last novel. The growth to moral maturity of a social nature forecast in *Their Wedding Journey* and consummated in *A Hazard of New Fortunes* is surpassed in thematic complexity by the treatment of vicarious satisfaction in and artistic self-responsibility for one's imaginative creations. Indeed, in this respect Howells' minor March narratives anticipate the more experimental works of John Barth, Robert Coover, Gilbert Sorrentino, Ronald Sukenick, and Kurt Vonnegut, who examine in their own time the creative responsibility for one's fiction.

Howells turned to the Marches two more times, in *Their Silver Wedding Journey* (1899) and in *Hither and Thither in Germany* (1920). Both are travel books, the former issued first in an expensively ornate gift edition, the latter being Howells' revision of the same manuscript into a more conventional guide. In each volume there is much romanticizing and searching for the picturesque, but at this stage and in these circumstances we must excuse it. In 1899 Basil and Isabel March were practicing the aesthetic in the one place where Howells had implied that it was apt, "recapturing the Europe of their youth" not in the New York slums but in Europe itself; and in 1920 Howells himself was safely fancying the European past, carefully omitting any reference from the earlier edition that would rankle the mood of Prohibition and of hate for Germany. Their children raised and their living secure, both the Marches and their creator Howells settle back to the comfortable romanticizing that had been illicit up to now.

Clara Marburg Kirk's description of how Howells "imagined himself a generation back in time as he prepared for publication this earlier account of Germany where he and his wife had spent many happy months"[18] suggests the second approach to the aesthetic-ethic split so dominant in the March stories. In addition to using it thematically in his fictions, Howells experienced his own career as an artist in such terms.

The studies by Clara M. Kirk, John K. Reeves, and William M. Gibson discuss Howells' initial experiments with the romantic versus the real, which in many cases parallel the Marches' ambivalence between the aesthetic and ethic.[19] But this problem pursued Howells as an artist far into his writing career. The novelist Mr. Twelvemough of *A Traveler from Altruria* whimsically verges toward the aesthetic-artistic in the face of real social problems, making for several delightfully funny scenes which parody his artistic self-concern as a writer of stories. In Howells' preface to the Library Edition of *A Hazard of New Fortunes,* moreover, we see this same artistic temperament in a much more serious light. Remembering the horrible and pathetic violence of the labor dispute in that novel, one is startled to meet the author's grateful boast, "Opportunely for me there was a great street-car strike in New York"[20] at the time he was collecting material for the book, and to see how ecstatically he gathers up his windfall. Although he has not forgotten the poor, "what is better, the poor have not forgotten themselves in violences such as offered me the material of tragedy and pathos in my story."[21]

This is Howells' dilemma: drawn in sympathy to the urban plight, as he undertakes its artistic expression he must search out and cultivate the most terrible acts of violence and suffering, admitting that "In my quality of artist I could not regret these," and indeed taking great pleasure in finding them.[22] One of Howells' frequent correspondents of the previous decade, Frank Norris, recognized the problem and argued that sympathy for one's own art subsumed any personal feeling the author might have for his original material:

It does not at all follow that the same artist would be moved to tears over the report of parallel catastrophes in real life. As an artist, there is every reason to suppose he would welcome the news with downright pleasure. It would be for him "good material." He would see a story in it, a good scene, a great character.[23]

This is Norris' formula for writing "The Novel with a 'Purpose,'" whereby dispassionate craftsmanship prevents any chance of runaway didacticism. Howells, however, had in the themes of his own novels found this same problem to be much more complex. Such delight in artistically useful misfortune is an old March family trait, dating back to the first wedding journey, which is purged, on the highest level of artistic self-responsibility, only with *An Open-Eyed Conspiracy* and "A Circle in the Water." Thus while Norris resolved the problem by flatly denying the validity of personal emotions at all, Howells more subtly synthesizes the elements of vicarious pleasure and personal responsibility into a more acceptable artistic posture. Finally, in the licitly detached sphere of European second-honeymooning, nostalgic romanticizing itself becomes at last the role of the Marches in *Their Silver Wedding Journey,* and of Howells himself in *Hither and Thither in Germany.*

Thus Howells' own experiences as a literary artist do parallel those of the Marches as his characters, but in a more complete manner than has been heretofore suggested:

MARCHES		HOWELLS
aesthetic vs. ethic in sightseeing North America	*Their Wedding Journey*	romanticism vs. realism in writing an American novel
aesthetic vs. ethic in organizing their prospect of New York City	*A Hazard of New Fortunes*	sympathy for suffering vs. artistic delight in it
experience responsibility for the product of their creative imaginations	minor works of 1890s	expands theme to encompass artistic responsibility
second honeymoon to recapture their youth in harmless aestheticizing of picturesque Europe—*Their Silver Wedding Journey*	European travel books	in 1920, nostalgia as "he prepares for publication this earlier account of Germany where he and his wife had spent many happy months" —*Hither and Thither in Germany*

The aesthetic-ethic theme, then, is a much larger concern in the works of William Dean Howells than simply a clue to his initial experiments with realism. It serves not only that function, but at the same time offers itself as a vehicle for the strong thematic development of his characters the Marches, and as an index to his own artistic experience as author of the Basil and Isabel March stories.

CHAPTER THREE

Kate Chopin's Awakening to Naturalism

IT is almost a critical commonplace to acknowledge that American naturalism, apart from the obvious French influences, was prepared for by the strain in American literature developing from romanticism to local color, and from there to a sterner realism. Malcolm Cowley is particularly clear on this point, hailing the local colorists as the first group the young naturalists could look back to "whose work seemed to represent the truth and could therefore serve as models to the new generation." Cowley studies Edward Eggleston, Edgar Watson Howe, and Joseph Kirkland as "three local writers from the Middle West who described their respective backgrounds with less sentiment and decorum than those from other sections," and therefore signalled a break with the past.[1] Local color, as a movement, did the groundwork by introducing more mundane themes into American literature. But these local colorists were not immune to some of the very same ideas that were to influence the later naturalists. Lars Ahnebrink records Eggleston's confession, in his article "Books that Have Helped Me," that the immediate influence on *The Hoosier Schoolmaster* was a reading of Hippolyte A. Taine's "Art in the Netherlands" with its maxims on the artist and his milieu.[2] Donald Pizer continues to trace other such influences on the pre-naturalists, including Thomas Sergeant Perry's evolutionary dictum that every artist

is bound by the necessity of building on the foundations that society is laying every day. Every apparently insignificant action of ours contributes its mote to the sum of circumstances which inspire the writer, whose vision may be dim or inaccurate, but who can see only what exists or may exist, and is limited by experience whether this be treated literally or be modified by the imagination. No writer can escape this limitation any more than he can imagine a sixth sense.[3]

Perry, George Pellew, and especially Hamlin Garland "asserted a historical relativism which demanded that modern art be interpreted and judged on the basis of its truthful representation of contemporary life."[4] In his critical work, *Crumbling Idols,* Garland "concluded that the local colorist was the only writer capable of capturing contemporary social and individual complexity, since he alone worked in close enough detail with an area he knew intimately."[5] Coining the term "veritism," Garland urged: "Write of those things of which you know most, and for which you care most. By doing so you will be true to yourself, true to your locality, and true to your time."[6]

Local color, with its new subjects and themes, brought to American literature a sterner realism,[7] a point where some critics prefer to place Kate Chopin.[8] The case of her progression from a romanticist to a professional writer of local color sketches has been documented by the few historical society studies of her and by the general treatments in the literary histories and handbooks.[9] But what now appears as her major work, *The Awakening,* was for fifty years ignored, almost as its original printing by a lesser known, experimental Chicago publisher caused a few weeks of mild scandal and then dropped from the scene. In the mid-fifties, two scholarly magazines resurrected it for their "Old Books" sections and gave it laudatory reviews,[10] but it was not until 1966 that Larzer Ziff gave it more than cursory attention in his *The American 1890's,*[11] and Stanley Kauffmann reviewed a new paperback edition for *The New Republic.*[12] Only since then, with partial thanks to feminist critics, has the novel enjoyed sustained attention.

There is a very attractive pattern in Kate Chopin's development as a writer that reflects in microcosm the larger movement in American literature from romanticism and local color to realism and naturalism, as a careful reading of her novel shows. It would be foolish to claim that Kate Chopin was the American girl Zola (as Frank Norris was once fashioned "the American boy Zola"), and attempts to construe *The Awakening* as "an American Bovary" have been equally unsuccessful. The book stands simply as an advance in American literature, and the areas of its achievement are clearly ones pioneered by naturalism. So many of the devices of the naturalistic novel are operative—influences of heredity and environment, exposure to a new and threatening environment which in turn brings out animal instincts, a frank treatment of those instincts, a descent on the social scale to find more vital life, the presence of an understanding man of science, and a solution like so many other naturalistic novels, where the central figure is at the conclusion swept up into the book's controlling images—that such consideration seems in order, particularly because Chopin's stories and novels reflect so clearly the general trend in American literature of that era. Her theme is a romantic imaginative awakening; the catalyst for it is drawn from the materials of local color; and her method of following the action is naturalistic.

Kate Chopin's protagonist in *The Awakening* is Edna Pontellier, but before discovering a thing about her, the reader learns, by indirection, much about her husband Leonce. Insensitive to the Spanish and French patois of their talking parrot, the lilting Creole of the resort people across the way, and the French impressionist music that pervades their Gulf-side retreat, he can merely reflect on the sum of it as "more noise."[13] Totally immune to the sensuosity of these images, he dismisses them as frivolous sentiment, as if Edna were an adolescent on the nether side of Howells' ethic and aesthetic. Seeing his wife frolicking in the surf with her new friend, Robert Lebrun, he remarks "What folly! to bathe at such an hour in such heat!" If he does not regard his wife outrightly as a child, he at least considers her "a valuable piece of personal property" (p. 4).

Opposed to the dull and insensitive Leonce Pontellier is the vital and vibrant Edna. Chopin's perfunctory introduction of the husband

Mr. Pontellier wore eye-glasses. He was a man of forty, of medium height and rather slender build; he stooped a little. His hair was brown and straight, parted on one side. His beard was neatly and closely trimmed. (p. 2)

is contrasted with her opening description of his wife:

Mrs. Pontellier's eyes were quick and bright; they were a yellowish brown, about the color of her hair. She had a way of turning them swiftly upon an object and holding them there as if lost in some inward maze of contemplation or thought. Her eyebrows were a shade darker than her hair. They were thin and almost horizontal, emphasizing the depth of her eyes. She was rather handsome than beautiful. Her face was captivating by reason of a certain frankness of expression and a contradictory subtle play of features. Her manner was engaging. (p. 7)

By reaction to the seaside environment, personal appearance and behavior, even relative depth of personality, an immediate contrast between the husband and the wife has been set up. Leonce is forever a New Orleans club man who most prefers other New Orleans club men, but who has at least the minimal sensitivity to regret that his wife "evinced so little interest in things which concerned him, and valued so little his conversation," and who takes the trouble to complain about "her inattention, her habitual neglect of the children." She in turn feels crushed under "an indescribable oppression." It is the nature of this oppression, and her reaction against it in the form of her "awakening," that determine the action of the novel.

Edna's personality, then, is fairly well established as the novel begins. Six years of marriage to Leonce, motherhood, and fashionable life in New Orleans have not resulted in any serious trouble, despite her basic incompatibility with such circumstances. But as the story opens she is for the first time in an entirely different, Creole, environment (an important condition for the experiment of naturalism), and "though she had married a Creole, was not thoroughly at home in the society of Creoles: never before had she been thrown so intimately among them" (p. 8). Most impressive is "their entire absence of prudery," and Edna soon reveals herself susceptible:

That summer at Grand Isle she began to loosen a little the mantle of reserve that had always enveloped her. . . . The excessive physical charm of the Creole had first attracted her, for Edna had a sensuous susceptibility to beauty. (p. 35)

Leonce has shown himself impervious to the nature of the environment, preferring New Orleans business to his own Creole heritage. But Edna is attracted by it, and by the young man that it so strongly characterizes, whose "eyes gathered in and reflected the light and languor of the summer day"—Robert Lebrun.

An affair begins at once, almost predictably, because Robert has been doing such things at Grand Isle since the age of fifteen and no one thinks anything of it. But Edna Pontellier is forever different from the crowd, and although the Creole women definitely offer an attractive release from prudery, they remain essentially "mother-women," one of the things she is definitely not. These women, although liberated from prudery and prone to accept flirtations unallowed in other quarters, still have "no difficulty in reconciling it with a lofty chastity which in the Creole women seems to be inborn and unmistakable" (p. 23). Edna's disposition, however, extends only so far as the welcomed liberation, and Robert is soon warned, "She is not one of us; she is not like us. She might make the unfortunate blunder of taking you seriously" (pp. 50–51)

Robert, however, perseveres, with a corresponding response from Edna: "A certain light was beginning to dawn dimly within her,—the light which, showing the way, forbids it." But her response has much larger implications than even the Creole women suspect, for, "In short, Mrs. Pontellier was beginning to realize her position in the universe as a human being, and to recognize her relations as an individual to the world within and about her" (p. 33). After years in New Orleans as the wife of Leonce Pontellier, years unproductive of such consequence, the new environment has triggered a true awakening, which Chopin compares directly to natural sources:

The voice of the sea is seductive; never ceasing, whispering, clamoring, murmuring, inviting the soul to wander for a spell in abysses of solitude, to lose itself in mazes of inward contemplation. (p. 34)

Edna's awakening and its controlling image are under way.

As the novel continues, Edna's progress is underscored by the image of the sea, which—rather than the animalistic properties in nature—has been made the metaphor for her sexual stirring. It makes her think of another image, this time "of a summer day in Kentucky, of a meadow that seemed as big as the ocean to the very little girl walking through the grass, which was higher than her waist." Even more explicitly, "She threw out her arms as if swimming when she walked, beating the tall grass as one strikes the water" (pp. 41–42). A companion questions her about these memories, and she continues:

"I felt as if I must walk on forever, without coming to the end of it. I don't remember whether I was frightened or pleased. I must have been entertained.

"Likely as not it was Saturday," she laughed; "and I was running away from prayers, from the Presbyterian service, read in a spirit of gloom by my father that chills me yet to think of." (p. 42)

Thus the link is made between her oppression, now dating back to even her childhood, and the new sense of freedom at Grand Isle. She recalls her adolescent infatuations: first a cavalry officer, then "a young gentleman who visited a lady on a neighboring plantation," and finally "the face and figure of a great tragedian." But the cavalry officer has drifted out of her life, and she accepts in turn "the realization that she herself was nothing, nothing, nothing to the engaged young man," although it remains "a bitter affliction to her." Her marriage to Leonce, instead of being the product of a fourth infatuation, is in fact her final and most significant act of repression:

The acme of bliss, which would have been a marriage with the tragedian, was not for her in this world. As the devoted wife of a man who worshipped her, she felt she would take her place with a certain dignity in the world of reality, closing the portals forever behind her upon the realm of romance and dreams. (p. 47)

But now, at Grand Isle, the old sense of infatuation and romance has been revived, and when on Monday mornings Leonce heads back to New

Orleans and the children are packed off to grandmother's, "It seemed to free her of a responsibility which she had blindly assumed and for which Fate had not fitted her" (p. 48). In one of Chopin's more famous stories, "The Dream of an Hour," a young wife responds to news of her husband's death with the discreetly made exclamation, "Free, free, free!" Edna Pontellier, in *The Awakening,* is being brought to the same point.

The expression of Edna's awakening takes various forms, including an exposure to the indispensable background music, to the same themes by Frederic Chopin cited in *The Damnation of Theron Ware.* But inevitably Edna's imagination returns to the sea:

When she heard it there came before her imagination the figure of a man standing beside a desolate rock on the seashore. He was naked. His attitude was one of hopeless resignation as he looked toward a distant bird winging its flight away from him. (p. 65)

At this stage, while the people of Grand Isle take to the water as though a native element, Edna has still been trying to learn to swim, for "A certain ungovernable dread hung about her when in the water, unless there was a hand near by that might reach out and reassure her." But she soon becomes "Like the little tottering, stumbling, clutching child, who of a sudden realizes its powers, and walks for the first time alone, boldly and with over-confidence." It is not long before "she wanted to swim far out, where no woman had swum before," and with the self-depreciating remark, "Think of the time I have lost splashing about like a baby!" she now turns to swimming in earnest, for "As she swam she seemed to be reaching out for the unlimited in which to lose herself" (p. 71).

Translated into physical terms, Edna is experiencing "the first-felt throbbings of desire" (p. 77), and Chopin observes that "She was blindly following whatever impulse moved her, as if she had placed herself in alien hands for direction, and freed her soul of responsibility" (p. 82). For the first time she actively questions her responsibility to her husband, and wonders how in the first place she had submitted to him. "She perceived that her will had blazed up, stubborn and resistant" (p. 79), and imagines that "she were being borne away from some anchorage which had held her fast, whose chains had been loosening—had snapped the night before when the mystic spirit was abroad, leaving her free to drift whithersoever she chose to set her sails" (p. 87). But the physical is constantly gaining ground on the imagistic, and her primary awareness is expressed in such terms. Her awareness is troubled and confused as she sees "with different eyes . . . the new conditions in herself that colored and changed her environment" (p. 102). But aware or not, she has been transformed; and as an essentially different person she must continue her life with Leonce Pontellier and with Robert Lebrun.

One of the great ironies of *The Awakening* is that just as Edna is primed for involvement with Robert, he suddenly leaves Grand Isle for a sojourn in Mexico. Edna, struggling with her new interests and desires, is suddenly and pathetically left alone and is forced to admit her passion has been roused. "The sentiment which she entertained for Robert in no way resembled that which she felt for her husband, or had ever felt, or ever expected to feel." Even her children are now subordinated; she explains to a friend:

"I would give up the unessential; I would give my money, I would give my life for my children; but I wouldn't give myself. I can't make it more clear; it's only something which I am beginning to comprehend, which is revealing itself to me." (p. 122)

But Robert has gone, for reasons which only later, in the climax of the novel, will be made clear. For now, Edna must return to New Orleans, to "the programme which Mrs. Pontellier had religiously followed since her marriage, six years before" (pp. 128-29).

Edna, however, is returning to the city a changed woman, and it is inevitable that she will not so easily fit into the old social pattern. Her revolt is first openly manifested in her refusal to accept "Tuesday visits," one of *"les convenances"* her husband insists that she observe "if we ever expect to get on and keep up with the procession." She no longer cares. Such tensions build until we find Edna storming through chambers, smashing vases, removing her wedding ring and flinging it on the carpet; she wishes to destroy all of this "alien world which had suddenly become antagonistic" while it is Robert who dominates her thoughts and longings. The world of New Orleans society and families "was not a condition of life which fitted her, and she could see in it but an appalling and hopeless ennui," divorced from "the taste of life's delirium" (p. 145).

With the violence apparently out of her system, Edna's revolt subsides into a simple plan of doing as she likes, but also resolving never to take another step backwards. Her best friend now is not a member of New Orleans society but an outcast from that society, the withdrawing pianist, Mlle Reisz. Refreshed by her candor, a feature notably lacking in the rest of the city crowd, Edna is pleased to have the Mademoiselle salute her as a fellow artist, a brave soul, a soul that dares and defies. As Edna reads a letter from Robert, Mlle Reisz obligingly plays Chopin.

Leonce Pontellier, of course, can't ignore the obvious change in his wife, but dismisses it as "some sort of notion in her head concerning the eternal rights of women." Edna in turn totally dismisses her husband, observing, "What should I do if he stayed home. We wouldn't have anything to say to one another." The developing theme is played in a minor mode with the visit of Edna's Kentucky colonel father, who once again insists on dominating her and seeing that her husband tries to do the same. Only when he eventually departs does his daughter feel free.

More knowing than Edna's father, her husband, or even Edna herself, is Doctor Mandelet. He "knew his Creole" enough to realize exactly what was happening to Edna. The man of science, "He knew his fellow-creatures better than most men; knew that inner life which so seldom unfolds itself to unannointed eyes" (pp. 183–84). He sees clearly what is happening, but he knows his milieu as well, and mutters to himself, "I hope it isn't Arobin. . . . I hope to heaven it isn't Alcée Arobin" (p. 184).

The introduction of Arobin signals a new development in the progress of Edna's awakening. Edna has become restless, for "it seemed to her as if life were passing by, leaving its promise broken and unfulfilled." She turns to a new set of friends, lower on the social scale than even Mlle Reisz, a Mrs. Highcamp and the young man of fashion she cultivates, Alcée Arobin. They all go to the horse races, where Edna gambles recklessly, and within a page or two she is helping herself to beer. "She wanted something to happen—something, anything," and to expedite the action complies. "When, a few days later, Alcée Arobin called for Edna in his drag, Mrs. Highcamp was not with him." Edna feels unfaithful, but not to her husband—"she was thinking of Robert Lebrun." Yet Robert is in Mexico, while Arobin is quite near in New Orleans, "appealing to the animalism that stirred impatiently within her." Far beyond the Chopin and cigarettes and even beer, she now drinks "liquor from the glass as a man would have done," and becomes more adamant in her quest for freedom and independence.

Things become more serious. To Edna's playful admission, "By all the codes which I am acquainted with, I am a devilishly wicked specimen of the sex," Mlle Reisz cautions with her own extended image: "The bird that would soar above the level plain of tradition and prejudice must have strong wings. It is a sad spectacle to see the weaklings bruised, exhausted, fluttering back to earth" (p. 217). The acquaintance with Arobin escalates to an affair with their first passionate kiss, and "It was the first kiss of her life to which her nature had really responded. It was a flaming torch that kindled desire" (p. 218).

With the affair under way, Edna feels confidence, and "Above all, there was understanding":

She felt as if a mist had been lifted from her eyes enabling her to look upon and comprehend the significance of life, that monster made up of beauty and brutality. But among the conflicting sensations which assailed her, there was none of shame or remorse. There was a dull pang of regret because it was not the kiss of love which had enflamed her, because it was not love which had held this cup of life to her lips. (p. 219)

She happily plans a twenty-ninth birthday party for herself, at her new little home, inviting many of her new friends and old ones from Grand Isle. Among them is Victor, the younger brother of Robert Lebrun, who of course reminds Edna of her distant lover. But when Victor drinks too much wine, dons a garland of roses, and makes playful advances, singing Robert's old love songs, Edna is revolted by the pagan spectacle. She is unnerved so as to smash her drinking glass, embarrass the company, and bring the proceedings of the evening to an end. But Victor, almost intuitively, has been right: she concludes the night with sexual intercourse with Arobin.

Mr. and Mrs. Pontellier respectively retain their perspectives on the "awakening." Leonce, before asking a thing about their own relationship or her relationship to their children, "begged her to consider first, foremost, and above all else, what people would say. He was not dreaming of scandal. . . . He was simply thinking of financial integrity" (p. 243). Edna Pontellier sees her adventures in different terms altogether:

There was with her a feeling of having descended in the social scale, with a corresponding sense of having risen in the spiritual. Every step which she took toward relieving herself from obligations added to her strength and expanion as an individual. She began to look with her own eyes; to see and to apprehend the deeper undercurrents of life. (p. 245)

Edna tells herself that she is in fact happier with her children now because she is a fuller, more complete person. But Arobin has played a role more consonant with a different type of development: "He had detected the latent sensuality, which unfolded under his delicate sense of her nature's requirements like a torpid, torrid, sensitive bloom" (pp. 272–73).

Edna is "awakened" sexually; her social world, however, has begun to collapse. Her close friend Mme Ratignolle confesses that she can no longer be seen visiting Edna, apologizing, "Of course, it wouldn't matter if Mr. Arobin had not such a dreadful reputation." But the greatest abandonment comes at the hands of someone Edna would never suspect. Earlier Mlle Reisz had warned her that Robert left for Mexico "because he loves you, poor fool, and is trying to forget you, since you are not free to listen to him or to belong to him" (p. 210). Now, upon his return, he is uneasy with Edna; and instead of frolicking at her heels as at Grand Isle, he now takes control himself, quite coldly so. He becomes grateful to leave, but not before he confesses to his moral control. He has resisted her:

"Why? Because you were not free; you were Leonce Pontellier's wife. I couldn't help loving you if you were ten times his wife; but so long as I went away from you and kept away I could help telling you so . . . . I realized what a cur I was to dream of such a thing, even if you had been willing." (pp. 280–82)

Edna protests that she is indeed willing, that she is no longer one of Pontellier's possessions. Away from Robert for a short time, she decides it is "better to wake up after all, even to suffer, rather than remain a dupe to illusions all one's life." She returns home to find that Robert has not waited. He has left a note: "I love you. Good-by—because I love you." He has awakened Edna to sexual experience and a whole new sensibility, but, unlike her, holds fast to his society's moral standard. And Edna is left by herself.

In the final chapter of the novel Edna is found, alone, back at Grand Isle, too early in the season for others to be there. Once again, she finds the sea seductive, and this time strips naked and walks into it. Assembling a collage of all the book's major images, Kate Chopin ends her novel by letting Edna be consumed by them.

The Awakening, highly praised by almost every critic to write on it, is not a direct imitation of Zola, nor is it a slavish exercise in the prescripts of the naturalistic method. Nearly all commentators now admit that the purely naturalistic American novel was never written—Norris resolving *McTeague* into romanticism, Dreiser infusing his characters with an idealism only partially vanquished, Kate Chopin describing a romantic awakening, but presenting it according to the tenets of naturalism. Race, moment, and milieu (here described as a local colorist would have them) are the catalysts of Edna's change—a change that is, moreover, tested as a Zolaesque experiment.

The final evidence that *The Awakening* was written in at least partially a naturalistic manner from Kate Chopin herself, in a letter to *Book News* helpfully reprinted by her first biographer, Daniel Rankin. Mrs. Chopin writes:

Having a group of people at my disposal, I thought it might be entertaining (to myself) to throw them together and see what would happen. I never dreamed of

Mrs. Pontellier making such a mess of things and working out her own damnation as she did. If I had the slightest intimation of such a thing I would have excluded her from the company. But when I found out what she was up to, the play was half over and it was then too late.[14]

Kate Chopin has described what happened in her own laboratory: the awakening of Edna Pontellier.

CHAPTER FOUR

Gatsby as Composition

His first novel was written for all the wrong reasons—as the autobiography of an eighteen-year-old, to celebrate his college adventures and coming of age, to seize upon popular controversy in a bid for bestsellerdom, to win the hand of Zelda Sayre—and so *This Side of Paradise* boasts the compositional sense of the autodidactic novel: omniscient narration, full and discursive characterization, the loose chronological structure of episode, and no real center of interest other than the fortunes of subject number one, the protagonist or author manqué.[1] F. Scott Fitzgerald's first attempt at fiction thus bears all the qualities of the noncompositional novel, written in naive imitation of history with scant evidence of the artist's finer hand.

Everything proceeds in the inevitable straight line, from Amory Blaine's birth, pampered childhood, first kiss, and adolescent crises. And here is the critical problem: Amory is so much the center of things that there is no machinery to evaluate what happens to him. Instead, the supposedly omniscient narrator (who should know better) participates in the dips and dives of Amory's romantic enthusiasms. Once the reader catches on, the technique (or rather lack of it) has some advantage, for the book literally composes itself as its protagonist grows. For most curricular adventures, Fitzgerald's naive manner is adequate. But then Amory falls in love, and the narrative falls to pieces. The cause is Rosalind Connage.

The first chapter of Book Two begins with stage directions for an event in the Connage house—more particularly, in "a large, dainty bedroom. . . . A girl's bedroom: pink walls and curtains and a pink bedspread on a cream-colored bed." After detailing the room and its contents for a while more, the narrator gushes, "One would enjoy seeing the bill called forth by the finery displayed and one is possessed by a desire to see the princess for whose benefit—Look! There's some one! Disappointment! This is only a maid hunting for something. . . ." (p. 179). The technique of stage directions is a legitimate device to build eagerness and anticipation, but all decorum is lost when "ROSALIND enters. ROSALIND is—utterly Rosalind. She is one of those girls who need never make the slightest effort to have men fall in love with them . . . but in the true sense she is not spoiled. Her fresh enthusiasms, her will to grow and learn, her endless faith in the inexhaustibility of romance, her courage and fundamental honesty—these things are not spoiled" (pp. 182–83). The young Fitzgerald has described a person equal to Eleanor Roosevelt, with a touch of Joan of Arc for flavoring, which holds together fine until she opens her mouth. "Oh, don't ask me," she replies to Amory's marriage proposal. "You know I'm old in some ways—in others—well, I'm just a little girl. I like sunshine and pretty things and cheerfulness—and I dread responsibility. I don't want to think about pots and kitchens and brooms. I want to worry whether my legs will get slick and brown when I swim in the summer" (p. 210).

Because there is no controlling logic to them, the elements of Fitzgerald's composition fall into disorder. The clear line of history has not proved adequate or appropriate to the tangle of human emotion encountered in the novel. The writer must find proper avenues down which to direct these emotions—or better yet, he must intuit their directions and lay the paving ahead of them, so that the reader can follow in comfortable pursuit. But Amory's romantic agony is too much his own; insufficient to spark a similar response in the reader, it leaves the narrator—the very embodiment of personal energy which holds and directs the book—floundering in confusion, having been cheaply seduced by a character he's supposed to control.

Jay Gatsby, of course, is a far more complex creation and one might suppose that Fitzgerald's ability to conceive of him implies a growth in artistic method. Yet the simple difference is that this latter novel is *composed*. There is more to the action than the simple line of history. Told from Nick Carraway's perspective of sorting out Gatsby's story, *The Great Gatsby* is put together like a jigsaw puzzle: time offering its contributions from past, present, and anticipated future, while the process of detection incorporates the spatial realm as well. How a bootlegger and petty extortionist can wind up being "worth the whole damn bunch put together," especially so valued by a conservative midwesterner, the stable center of the novel with whom the reader explicitly identifies, is a matter of no small complexity. The answer only makes sense for us because it is composed before our eyes, assembled by Nick Carraway in a manner which reflects Fitzgerald's greater art in designing the novel.

Two and one-half chapters—48 pages of a 182 page novel—are spent waiting for Gatsby. Rumors abound, anticipation mounts, while all Nick has is a late-night glimpse of Gatsby's figure quaking at the water's edge. Then, at one of Gatsby's monster parties, Carraway comes face to face with the man himself:

> He smiled understandingly—much more than understandingly. It was one of those rare smiles with a quality of eternal reassurance in it, that you may come across four or five times in a life. It faced—or seemed to face—the whole external world for an instant, and then concentrated on *you* with an irresistible prejudice in your favor. It understood you just as far as you wanted to be understood, believed in you as you liked to believe in yourself, and assured you that it had precisely the impression of you that, at your best, you hoped to convey.

Are Nick's enthusiasms running amok, like the narrator's in *This Side of Paradise?* If so, it might be excusable—Nick is after all a character as well as the spokesman, and he would be subject to the same fallibilities as the writer's other creations. But the writer himself must keep control, and Fitzgerald does this by making the scene dramatic, showing Nick being seduced and then catching himself just in time:

> Precisely at that point it vanished—and I was looking at an elegant young roughneck, a year or two over thirty, whose elaborate formality of speech just missed being absurd. (p. 48)

And so Nick's portrait of Gatsby is a composition *in process.* It is not makeshift, it is a finished product, but one which captures the essence of the artist's act—much like the action painting of abstract expressionists. Fitzgerald's choice of method is especially apt for the style of Gatsby's character and is the reason why the book succeeds, as well as serving as a reminder of why *This Side of Paradise* fails.

Because Gatsby is so much a self-created person, his relative stature in time and space is of great importance. The first half of Fitzgerald's novel offers nothing of hard substance, just rumor and speculation and teasingly brief encounters with Gatsby. The image is there, of course, but it has not yet come into focus—Fitzgerald reserves that pleasure for the reader, whose experience will replicate Nick's in coming to grips with Gatsby.

It is the second half of *The Great Gatsby,* chapters six through nine, that finally gets down to basic facts about the man, but not before announcing that our own attempts to intuit his background and growth of character have been misguided. "The truth was that Jay Gatsby of West Egg, Long Island," we are finally told, "sprang from his Platonic conception of himself'' (p. 99). Hence there are three distinct processes of composition before us: Fitzgerald writing the novel at large, Nick Carraway assembling the bits and pieces of Gatsby's career, and Jay Gatsby in the act of inventing himself. By the novel's end, all three have become master fictionists. With so much emphasis on the forms of composition, time and space *as components* become the center of interest, in place of the historical line Fitzgerald depended upon in his first novel.

Reinforcing this compositional design, the matter of time and space develops into the novel's theme. Gatsby has not only composed a portrait of himself, but has built a world he hopes to inherit—of stature, taste, and class, all keyed to the memory of Daisy Buchanan. But his vision of Daisy has grown in the studio of his ambitions for five years, beyond all contact with the real Daisy. ''Almost five years!'' Nick is forced to exclaim. ''There must have been moments even that afternoon when Daisy tumbled short of his dreams—not through her own fault, but because of the colossal vitality of his illusion.'' Fitzgerald has become a good enough artist to appreciate that he is no longer dealing with history, and so the historical line of action must be replaced with something else. Nick knows what has happened. ''No amount of fire or freshness can challenge what a man will store up in his ghostly heart'' (p. 97). So much of Gatsby has gone into loving the idea of Daisy that to live himself, he must obliterate the past. But Gatsby's dreams are ideal, while Daisy is too pitifully real. ''He knew that when he kissed this girl, and forever wed his unutterable visions to her perishable breath,'' we are told, ''his mind would never romp again like the mind of God'' (p. 112). Fitzgerald has solved his problem of writing a novel by making its very theme the problematics of artistic creation.

Why does Gatsby fail, when Fitzgerald achieves so much success with the same methods? The reason is his dependency upon Daisy as a love object, a dependency which the narrator of *This Side of Paradise* so fatefully shared. ''He hadn't once ceased looking at Daisy,'' Nick informs us, ''and I think he revalued everything in his house accordingly to the measure of response it drew from her well-loved eyes'' (p. 92). Gatsby's self-sustaining idealism has been routed through a new window of perception—Daisy's approbation. The greatness of Gatsby shares the limits of its source, Jay's love for an object unequal to his idealism. ''So the whole caravansary had fallen in like a card house at the disapproval in her eyes'' (p. 114).

When Tom Buchanan sets out to destroy Gatsby, he strikes to the core of Gatsby's being: his compositional sense of time and space. Facing off in the New York hotel room, Gatsby and Buchanan aim their first attacks at each other's weaknesses. Jay forces Daisy to say she never loved Tom. "Not at Kapiolani?" Tom demands. "I can't help what's past," Daisy sobs to Gatsby. "I did love him once—but I loved you too." Seeing Gatsby's idealism weaken in the face of time's reality, Buchanan interrupts. "Why—they're things between Daisy and me that you'll never know, things that neither of us can forget." Tom has found a point of weakness, part of the makeup of Gatsby's soul. As Nick observes, "The words seems to bite physically into Gatsby" (p. 133). All that remains is Gatsby's spatial substance, the sources of his wealth and character. "He and this Wolfsheim bought up a lot of side-street drugstores here and in Chicago and sold grain alcohol over the counter," Tom reveals. "That's one of his little stunts. I picked him for a bootlegger the first time I saw him, and I wasn't far wrong." With this, Daisy slips from Gatsby. "With every word she was drawing further and further into herself, so he gave that up, and only the dead dream fought on as the afternoon slipped away, trying to touch what was no longer tangible, struggling unhappily, undespairingly, toward that lost voice across the room" (pp. 134–35).

Fitzgerald's choice of a compositional character for Gatsby is the key to this novel's success, just as the lack of such complexity, where needed, doomed *This Side of Paradise* to the status of apprenticeship work, if not outright failure. In that first novel, no variety of expositional technique—paragraph snapshots, dramatic interludes, stage directions, reading lists, pasted-in letters—could deflect the action from its staid historical line. There was little else to say about Amory Blaine, because Fitzgerald had nothing else to see. But Gatsby is much more interesting a character, and that interest is made available to the reader by the depth and play of his composition, all of which happens right in the reader's presence. Gatsby's depth makes plausible the complexity of Nick Carraway's narration—reporting some of the action as his own eyewitness account, but resorting elsewhere to the reports of others, reconstructions from second- and third-hand sources, and finally, in the best piece of writing Fitzgerald ever produced, to the finely detailed account of Gatsby's death, which is created entirely in Nick's imagination.

That imagination has been charged with a novel's worth of experience with Jay Gatsby. No longer the person we met on page one, Nick has been vitalized by Gatsby, turned into a creative manipulator of time and space by a model who made himself in such terms. Therefore, Gatsby cannot be said to fail, even in terms of the novel's plot. For although Jay Gatsby has been robbed of his dream and his life, Nick Carraway has inherited his gift to create. And it is not a private gift, but instead becomes Nick's ability to tell Gatsby's story, to write the novel we are now reading. The rich techniques of that novel—the complex narration, the time shifts, the lush but appropriate symbolism—spring from the very character of Gatsby and from Nick's artistic manner of capturing it.

Did Fitzgerald see himself in Gatsby? That speculation is deliberately left open—witness the novel's last page, where Gatsby's quest is ultimately compared to life's quest against death, a vision large enough to take in author and reader alike. If Fitzgerald did see himself so, it is to his credit that he handles the identification in a manner more deft than the adolescent posing in *This Side of Paradise* (which, after all, bore the working title, "The Romantic Egotist," retained as the subtitle to Book One). A more fruitful comparison is between Fitzgerald and the Buchanans. He is definitely not one of them, an amazing growth of insight for a writer who only a few years before had written what he hoped to be a formula best-seller so he might buy his way into the monied classes, and who had made the characters Anthony and Gloria Patch (of the *Beautiful and the Damned*) seem stupidly modeled on the Scott and Zelda created by the first novel's success.

The shallower aspects of Scott and Zelda are present in *The Great Gatsby*—not in direct portrayal, but in Nick's final judgment of them. "They were careless people, Tom and Daisy," Nick tells us near the end, "they smashed up things and creatures and then retreated back into their money or their vast carelessness, or whatever it was that kept them together, and let other people clean up the mess they had made" (pp. 180-81). Like everything else in this masterful novel, Nick's opinion is not laid on, but rather grows from the compositional manner of the story. His ability to make this judgment, against the Buchanans and in favor of the problematic Gatsby, signals his growth to the stature of a man of full imagination. It is a sign of Fitzgerald's growth as well.

Faulkner's Community:
Thematic Unity in *Knight's Gambit*

WILLIAM FAULKNER was particular about his short story collections. Unlike some writers who might allow a publisher to assemble at random anything written since the last collection, Faulkner insisted that a short story volume should have "form" and "integration" equal to that of a novel, and at best should be "an entity of its own, single, set for one pitch, contrapuntal in integration, toward one end, one finale."[1] *Knight's Gambit,* however, at one time intended by Faulkner to be part of the highly acclaimed *Collected Stories* of 1950,[2] has been treated with condescension by the reviewers[3] and scorn by the critics,[4] and is still considered a careless and disjunctive piece of work.

Many readers of *Knight's Gambit* have been satisfied to describe it as a collection of Gavin Stevens stories.[5] But knowing Faulkner's concern for integrity, the mere presence of a single character in several tales would be the shallowest of reasons for fusing them into one volume. It is likely that a larger thematic concern, relevant to Faulkner's greater works, drew these stories together, and that Faulkner had a more artistic reason for collecting them than furnishing for scholars a systematic record of his experiments with the character of Gavin Stevens. Stevens is a constant, but so is the community of which he is a part. The real theme of these stories is shown by the various outsiders to that community and the community's reaction to them. As outsiders they are by no means monolithic: here Faulkner enriches his theme by presenting not just the traditional and all too expectable Yankee intruder, but outsiders from other regional, national, and international areas, and in some stories "outsiders" from within the very heart of the community itself, figures who express by symbol or hyperbole some of that community's most central ideas, and who allow Faulkner the scope for statements on man more

Reprinted by permission from *Critique* 11(2) 1969, pp. 81–100.

characteristic of his greater work. But by narrowly and unnaturally focusing on Stevens, the reader is actually drawn to the least satisfying aspects of many of the stories. After all, *Knight's Gambit* is a separate book, and only when read as such does it make sense.

"Smoke," although described as one of Faulkner's least effective stories, was apparently one of his favorite shorter pieces. He submitted it to magazines five times before it was finally published in *Harper's* for April of 1932, and two years later he collected it in *Doctor Martino*.[6] In 1949 Faulkner intended to integrate it into the *Collected Stories* volume, but he eventually used it as the lead story in the *Knight's Gambit* collection, the only story therein which had been previously collected.[7] In addition to attending so persistently to its publication, Faulkner offered "Smoke" to CBS television, where Gore Vidal and Robert Mulligan adapted it to win a 1954 "best television play" award.[8]

Why then do the Faulkner scholars dismiss the work? Perhaps the best way to make "Smoke" look bad is to read it as a Gavin Stevens–Chick Mallison story, as the critics invariably do. Stevens is there, but entirely in the second (and inferior) half of the story, after the first descriptive section has abruptly fallen away and the reader is left with twenty-four pages of assertive ratiocination. The entire story is told by a narrator who has been present at the events, but with no indication that he might be Stevens' nephew. Instead, the narrator associates himself with the community, continually remarking that "we believed" and "we were not surprised." The narrator is emphatically one of "we in Jefferson"—the community of people who form the frame of the story.

Within this frame, and before the people, is enacted the drama of Anselm Holland, a crass and violent "outlander" who belongs neither to this nor to any recognizable community. The first words of the story compress years of observed action:

Anselm Holland came to Jefferson many years ago. Where from, no one knew. But he was young then and a man of parts, or of presence at least, because within three years he had married the only daughter of a man who owned two thousand acres of some of the best land in the country, and he went to live in his father-in-law's house, where two years later his wife bore him twin sons and where a few years later still the father-in-law died and left Holland in full possession of the property, which was now in his wife's name. But even before that event, we in Jefferson had already listened to him talking a trifle more than loudly of "my land, my crops"; and those of us whose fathers and grandfathers had been bred here looked upon him a little coldly and a little askance for a ruthless man and (from the tales told about him by both white and Negro tenants and by others with whom he had dealings) for a violent one. (p. 3)

Old Anse is the usurping outlander, appropriating to himself a rich part of the community. However, his twin sons, young Anse and Virginius, are respected as rightful members of the community as was their mother, and no one is "surprised" when old Anse refuses to surrender to them the land he has held in trust. He antagonizes young Anse by wasting and mistreating "the land which his mother aimed for him and Virginius to have," and finally by committing a deed the community-narrator calls "what to men of our town and time and thinking was the unpardonable outrage . . . digging up the graves in the family cemetery where his wife's people rested, among them the grave in which his wife had lain for thirty years" (p. 4).

Possession of the land, from the community's point of view, becomes the center of the action. But not mere physical possession—this is the difference between the two "murderers" of old Anse Holland. Young Anse, who found his father desecrating the graves and felled him with what he thought was a mortal blow, wanted not financial gain from the land, but simply to have the land "which had been his mother's and in which her bones now lie . . . be treated right." With this accomplished, "it was all vindicated then . . . the outrage, the injustice, the lost good name, and the penitentiary stain—all gone now like a dream." Virginius would be welcome to both halves, just as long as the usurped property would be back in the right hands. Granby Dodge, however, desires the land for financial gain, and so he murders old Anse (after young Anse has left him for dead), has the probate judge killed by a Memphis thug, and plots the murder of Virginius.

Gavin Stevens eventually performs the office of transposing the law to fit the principles of local community justice. But the probate judge himself is the primary understander of local right, for he possesses "that sort of probity and honor which has never had time to become confused and self-doubting with too much learning in the law . . . the one man among us who believed that justice is fifty per cent legal knowledge and fifty per cent unhaste and confidence in himself and in God (p. 11). He has "little knowledge of the law and a great deal of hard common sense," and the people of the community vote for him "with a kind of childlike confidence and trust." Pure abstract justice is as dangerous as "disease germs." Because Judge Dunkinfield has refused to make the legally obvious but communally false judgment against young Anse, Granby Dodge has the judge murdered.

At this point, Gavin Stevens enters to help clear up the whole matter. The story falls neatly in half as Faulkner turns from the judge, sitting in his chair as dead as Hawthorne's Judge Pyncheon, to the *in medias res* of "It took Gavin Stevens a long time, that day—he and the little brass box." Stevens points out what is inherent in the story of the Holland family: that young Anse has nothing to gain from murdering his father, that the land will eventually return if the community waits long enough, and that young Anse is used to waiting. The man who cannot wait, however, is Granby Dodge, who wants the land for private, not communal or patrimonial, use. Thus while legality might interpret young Anse's rash and probably self-defensive blow as self-motivated murder, Stevens' investigation leads to the more locally correct solution.

A successful Gavin Stevens–Chick Mallison story would center on Stevens' perception and the boy's reaction to it. In "Smoke" there is little of the sort. Instead of Chick watching his Uncle, we have the community watching an intruder. In the place of Stevens' moral drama, we see the pageant of Anselm Holland, his two sons, and "two thousand acres of some of the best land in the country." Gavin Stevens, "a Harvard graduate . . . among the squatting men . . . talking to them in their idiom," might well be the liaison between the outside world and this particular community, but his role as such is minimized in this story. To the jury foreman he explains not so much the motivations of Anse and his sons as the flaw in Granby Dodge's crime, and only an outside interest in Gavin Stevens would make this epilogue the center of the story.

"Monk," published in *Scribner's* for May of 1937, represents a clear advancement over the technical problems of "Smoke." Gavin Stevens' role is more organic to the action, and the narrator is even briefly identified as Stevens' nephew (p. 46), but both are thematically subordinated to the tale of another outlander, Stonewall Jackson "Monk" Oldethrop. Monk comes from an isolated part of the narrator's county, "a country which twenty-five years ago (Monk was about twenty-five) was without roads almost and where even the sheriff of the county did not go." A society by itself, it is

a country impenetrable and almost uncultivated and populated by a clannish people who owned allegiance to no one and no thing and whom outsiders never saw until a few years back when good roads and automobiles penetrated the green fastnesses where the denizens with their corrupt Scotch-Irish names intermarried and made whiskey and shot at all strangers from behind log barns and snake fences. (p. 40)

Monk is not only physically removed from conventional society, but is mentally isolated in a striking way. Abandoned as an infant, he spends the first six years of his life with his grandmother, "an old woman who lived like a hermit, even among those fiercely solitary people." Things become too quiet, however, and when members of the community step in to investigate, they face little Monk, struggling with a shotgun to defend the grandmother's rotting corpse. The child himself escapes, but "they knew that he was somewhere watching them while they prepared the body for burial . . . and on the following Sunday they found where he had been digging into the grave, with sticks and with his bare hands." Monk grows up in the care of the moonshiner Fraser, and accords the old man "the absolute and unquestioning devotion of a dog." After Monk reaches his twenties Fraser dies, and when "the man, whoever it was, came along in the truck or the car and said, 'All right, Monk. Jump in,' he got into it exactly as the homeless dog would have, and came to Jefferson."

In Jefferson, Monk allegedly commits the crime that sends him to a life sentence at the state penitentiary. But even before being told of the crime, we learn that

He was a moron, perhaps even a cretin; he should never have gone to the penitentiary at all. But at the time of his trial we had a young District Attorney who had his eye on Congress, and Monk had no people and no money and not even a lawyer, because I don't believe he ever understood why he should need a lawyer or even what a lawyer was, a young man just admitted to the bar, who probably knew but little more about the practical functioning of criminal law than Monk did, who perhaps pleaded Monk guilty at the direction of the court or maybe forgot that he could have entered a plea of mental incompetence, since Monk did not for one moment deny that he had killed the deceased. (pp. 39–40)

Monk's desire to admit the crime is perplexing: "They could not keep him from affirming or even reiterating it, in fact." But "He was neither confessing nor boasting"; Monk can't remember who he supposedly killed, and is willing to confess to the murder of anybody, even of people presently alive and in the courtroom. The murder itself was "as though the sound of the shot had broken the barrier behind which he had lived for twenty-five years and that he had now crossed the chasm into the world of living men by means of the dead body at his feet." Thus he raises his "eager, sympathetic voice" to his new-found friends: the deputy, the jailer, and the judge. But Monk fails to communicate even here, and is carried off to the penitentiary "hermetically sealed" within a railroad coach.

Gavin Stevens enters the story when he learns from the confession of a dying drunkard that Monk had been framed. Stevens arranges a pardon, but Monk, predictably, refuses it: "He was a trusty now; he had transferred to the warden the same doglike devotion which he had given to old Fraser." But the complexity in which Gavin Stevens participates occurs a week later when Monk, apparently trying to lead a jailbreak, ruthlessly kills his beloved warden. Stevens must face the perplexity of such an act by a man who begged to remain in jail to finish knitting his warden's sweater; but almost immediately he can explain to Chick why Monk has so behaved. "Because he had no conception of death," Stevens tells his nephew. "I don't believe he had ever connected the carrion at his feet behind the filling station that night with a man who had just been walking and talking, or that on the ground in the compound with the man for whom he was knitting the sweater." Such is the lasting barrier between Monk and human communication: he cannot comprehend the murder of his own kind.

Stevens does not have to investigate to determine this fact about Monk's alienation. What Stevens does investigate, and what forms the second, ratiocinative section of the story, is the implication of Monk's final words on the gallows: "And now I am going out into the free world, and farm." In this unnecessarily long and less interesting part of the story, Stevens finds that a "troublemaking" convict, himself framed into a murder, has taken advantage of Monk's simplicity to convince him that the one thing preventing "all us poor ignorant country folks" from walking out into the free world and farming it is the want of a pistol to force a way past the warden. Terrel, the convict, is speaking metaphorically: he's not a farmer, but a filling-station operator. Monk, in his simplicity of primary associations, lives the metaphor. He kills the warden so that he can "walk out into the free world and farm it"—or, once again, to attempt a communication.

Stevens' detective work is a minor part of the tale. It is enhancing to Monk's story that Stevens can make explicit what he already knows in the first half, and that he can do it by revealing one more misuse of poor, simple Monk. But the heart of the work is not Stevens' ratiocination. "Monk" is most successfully read as the story of another outlander in relation to the community. Here the dilemma is one of communication itself. Stevens' function is subordinate to Monk's story; there is no organic justification for having it the other way around. At one point Gavin Stevens is chided by the governor for being so pained at the injustice of the case; Stevens merely walks out of the prison, glad to be out of "the smell and the taste of where he had been." Perhaps, regarding the significance Gavin Stevens is to have in the later novels, one might want to spotlight this passage as a significant step in his education and development. But to the reader of these stories as an integral volume, focusing on Stevens makes the rest of the story seem irrelevant. The first paragraph indicates the narrative's force:

I will have to try to tell about Monk. I mean, actually try—a deliberate attempt to bridge the inconsistencies in his brief and sordid and unoriginal history, to make something out of it, not only with the nebulous and inexplicable material which he left behind him. Because it is only in literature that the paradoxical and even mutually negativing anecdotes in the history of a human heart can be juxtaposed and annealed by art into verisimilitude and credibility. (p. 39)

To what extent does Gavin Stevens "make something out of it"? Midway through, he enters and makes explicit and assertive what has been described before. But this would hardly make his the central action of the story. Stevens works with the strong thematic material of the outlander and his attempt at communication, and this theme, when properly understood, makes sense of the story.

"Hand Upon the Waters" might seem to be the detective story that "Smoke" and "Monk" are not. After a three-page dramatization of a drowning, Gavin Stevens spends seventeen pages "solving" the murder. But the particulars of the "murder case" make the story something much more. Yoknapatawpha County, we are told, "had been founded not by one pioneer but by three simultaneous ones." The family of the first, the Holstons, had died out before the end of the nineteenth century, but a descendent of the second, the Greniers, had survived down to that day. However,

the Louis Grenier, whose dead face Stevens was driving eight miles in the heat of a July afternoon to look at, had never known he was Louis Grenier. He could not even spell the Lonnie Grinnup he called himself . . . living year in and year out, in the hovel he had built himself. (p. 66)

Lonnie Grinnup, a self-determined outcast from the community, is figuratively the vital center of the community in exile, and even "his hut and trotline and fishtrap were in almost the exact center of the thousand and more acres his ancestors had once owned. But he never knew it." Gavin Stevens, however, does know it, and for a particular reason. He, Stevens, has become "a hundred years afterwards" the one surviving representative of the three founding names. He realizes that while "as county attorney he had no business there, even if it had not been an accident," he still must go "to look at the dead man's face for a sentimental reason." It is the sentimental reason that takes Gavin Stevens out of his role as county attorney–detective and places him within the community theme common to the *Knight's Gambit* stories. Stevens, in "Hand Upon the Waters," becomes organic to the theme, and his new role makes for a more satisfying story. Unlike "Smoke" and "Monk," where he acts only at the end, almost as an intellect *deus ex machina,* he is here a much more integral part of the story. He is present in the áction, and reacts to it. Toward the end of the tale he is nearly killed himself. Because of his intimate connection with Lonnie—their common basis of community ancestry—his detective work is infused with a larger meaning. And like Nick Carraway in F. Scott Fitzgerald's *The Great Gatsby,* he is given a compositional role—but only in relation to the theme of community.

"Tomorrow" is still another story about the people, the community, and "outsiders" of various degrees. Significantly, there is no break-away division as in the previous pieces. The sentence "Uncle Gavin had not always been county attorney," recalling the divisional "It took Gavin Stevens a long time that day" of "Smoke" and the "Inquest? Stevens said" of "Hand Upon the Waters," is in fact the very first line of "Tomorrow." The story details, rather than being presented before Stevens' entry, are developed simultaneously with his own action. The story begins with Stevens' defense of a man named Bookwright, who has killed "a swaggering bravo calling himself Buck Thorpe . . . kinless, who had appeared overnight from nowhere, a brawler, a gambler." Thorpe has seduced and abducted Bookwright's daughter, a minor, and Stevens can understand Bookwright's act. But Stevens must come to understand the action of Jackson Fentry, the one man on the jury who refused to acquit Bookwright. Just why Fentry won't "vote Mr. Bookwright free" becomes the subject of Stevens' inquiry.

Stevens' action is more properly an inquiry, rather than an act of detection or ratiocination. Instead of putting things together, he asks and is quite plainly told just what happened to Fentry and why he cannot properly acquit Bookwright. Stevens and his nephew Chick (who is named for the first time in this story) must journey "to the very other end of the county" to learn the details about Fentry. The Fentry home itself is barren and isolated, and Jackson's elderly father, G. A., drives the two off with his shotgun. Stopping down the road at the Pruitts', Stevens is told how the Fentrys have been keeping themselves apart from people for years. The root of it all? Pruitt comments on the essential loneliness of Jackson Fentry's life even before the crucial incident, living from dawn to dusk

the life his grandpa led until he died between the plow handles one day, and that his pa would lead until he died in a corn furrow, and then it would be his turn, and not even no son to come and pick him up out of the dirt. (p. 92)

Finally Fentry leaves the farm for a sawmill job, returning two and one-half years later with a baby. Retaining a Negro hand to help his father farm, Fentry single-handedly raises the child, "doing the cooking and washing and nursing that baby, milking the goat to feed it.'' Refusing all offers of assistance, he stitches the boy's clothes by hand, and even fashions a satchel to carry him into the fields. One day, however, the child disappears, and since then the Fentrys have kept severely alone.

Heading back to town, Gavin and Chick are hailed by Isham Quick, whose father owned the sawmill where Fentry worked. Quick knows where the child came from, where he went, and why Fentry voted against Bookwright. During his last winter at the mill Fentry sheltered a deserted, eight-month pregnant young woman, who consented to marry him just before she died in childbirth. He returned home with the child, as Rufus Pruitt has told, and raised it until the woman's kin came to repossess the child. Although the two brothers had the law on their side, Quick observes "that wasn't the first time it ever occurred to me that this world ain't run like it ought to be run a heap more times than it is.'' He follows the brothers to the inevitable scene with Fentry, where they take back their kin. Fentry and the boy pathetically fight the separation, but the battle is lost before it was begun, for "They got the law.'' Fentry's collapse is complete, "like all his bones had run to water,'' in the face of the undeniable claim, "It's the law.'' The money offered for boarding the boy he limply tosses aside.

The final answer to Stevens' inquiry comes when Quick tells how the Buck Thorpe that Bookwright has slain is the now-grown boy that was taken from Fentry years ago. "Of course he wasn't going to vote Bookwright free,'' says Quick; Bookwright had killed his "son.'' The story concludes with an emphasis on Stevens' breadth of understanding. Chick insists that under the same conditions he still would have freed Bookwright, "because Buck Thorpe was bad'':

"No, you wouldn't,'' Uncle Gavin said. He gripped my knee with one hand even though we were going fast, the yellow light beam level on the yellow road, the bugs swirling down into the light beam and ballooning away. "It wasn't Buck Thorpe, the adult, the man. He would have shot that man as quick as Bookwright did, if he had been in Bookwright's place. It was because somewhere in that debased and brutalized flesh which Bookwright slew there still remained, not the spirit maybe, but at least the memory, of that little boy, that Jackson and Longstreet Fentry, even though the man the boy had become didn't know it, and only Fentry did. And you wouldn't have freed him either. Don't ever forget that. Never.'' (pp. 104–5)

This story, the fourth in the volume, figures as an episode in the development of Gavin Stevens and education of Chick Mallison. But the point of education concerns the community-outlander-alienation theme. Buck Thorpe, the violent outlander, is in reality the "lost son'' of a lonely, isolated member of the community. Thus while Thorpe abducts one member of the community, and dies for it, Fentry attempts to effect community justice for his death. On another level, outside justice would hang Bookwright as it had deemed right the repossession of Fentry's child. By community standards, however, the opposite prevails. Bookwright goes free, and Fentry's loss is mourned.

"An Error in Chemistry," like "Smoke," was an award-winning story. The editors of *Ellery Queen's Mystery Magazine,* selecting it for the second prize in their annual story contest, described it as a tale "of almost pure detection."[9] To view it as a detective story, however, does little justice to its thematic materials: the outlander and the community. As in other stories in this volume, "An Error in Chemistry" has its location "twenty-odd miles into the remote back-country" where old Wesley Pritchel lives in alienation from the community. But the community itself first must bear an intruder, and Joel Flint fulfills the role in a classic manner:

He was the foreigner, the outlander, the Yankee who had come into our country two years ago as the operator of a pitch—a lighted booth where a roulette wheel spun against a bank of nickel-plated pistols and razors and watches and harmonicas, in a traveling street carnival—and who when the carnival departed had remained, and two months later was married to Pritchel's only living child: the dim-witted spinster of almost forty who until then had shared her irascible and violent-tempered father's almost hermit-like existence on the good though small farm which he owned. (p. 109)

Flint has "a voice lazy with anecdotes of the teeming outland which his listeners had never seen," and was, in opposition to the rural yet stable folk of the community, "a dweller among the cities, though never from his own accounting long resident in any one of them." But most importantly, for the plot of the story, Flint dramatizes his literal outlandishness by "one definite personal habit by which he presently became known throughout the whole county, even by men who had never seen him":

This was a harsh and contemptuous derogation, sometimes without even provocation or reason or opportunity, of our local southern custom of drinking whiskey by mixing sugar and water with it. He called it effeminacy, a pap for children, himself drinking even our harsh, violent, illicit and unaged homemade corn whiskey without even a sip of water to follow it. (p. 110)

The community for several years wonders at the doings out at the Pritchel place, although communication is sparse, the old man "having already druv the whole human race away from his house." One day, however, Flint telephones the sheriff that he's murdered his wife, and the action of the story begins. By the end, the reader has learned that "Joel Flint" has been simply the final role of a circus illusionist, Signor Canova, who has murdered the girl, her father, and the fictitious Joel Flint himself in order to sell the Pritchel farm for his own gain.

Gavin Stevens, one might anticipate, would be the one to solve the mystery. A superficial reading might give this impression, since Stevens is present, observing, throughout the story. And with *Ellery Queen's* hailing the story as a display "of almost pure detection" the case for lawyer-detective Stevens would appear to be made. The detection, however, is not on Stevens' part. The reader remembers that the entire community characterized Flint by his scorn for the local custom of cold toddies. When, disguised as old Wesley Pritchel, he mixes one, his is not only an ironic mistake, but, in this community, a very blatant one:

He unstoppered the decanter and poured whiskey into the three tumblers and set the decanter down and looked about the table. "You, boy," he said, "hand me the water bucket. It's on the back gallery shelf." Then, as I turned and started toward the door, I saw him reach and take up the sugar bowl and plunge the spoon into the sugar and then I stopped too. And I remember Uncle Gavin's and the sheriff's faces and I could not believe my eyes either as he put the spoonful of sugar into the raw whiskey and started to stir it. Because I had not only watched Uncle Gavin, but Uncle Gavin's father too who was my grandfather, and my own father before he died, and all the other men who would come to Grandfather's house who drank cold toddies as we called them, and even I knew that to make a cold toddy you do not put the sugar into the whiskey because sugar will not dissolve in raw whiskey but only lies in a little intact swirl like sand at the bottom of the glass; that you first put the water into the glass and dissolve the sugar into the water, in a ritual almost; then you add the whiskey, and that anyone like Old Man Pritchel who must have been watching men make cold toddies for nearly seventy years and had been making and drinking them himself for at least fifty-three, would know this too. (p. 127)

The recognition—the detection—is not made simply by Gavin Stevens, but by any and every member of the community present, and in particular by the narrator, Chick Mallison, who has been consistently characterized as one of the watching community. Violating a "ritual" of the community has attracted general attention, and it does again here. Only here it solves a murder mystery.

Once again the themes of the community and the outlander have contributed to the construction of this story. Gavin Stevens concludes by commenting on the character of Signor Canova, the gifted illusionist who "could not have helped obeying it [his gift] if he had wanted to."

Stevens moralizes as if Canova had been Ethan Brand, theorizing, "What else could the possession of such a gift as his have engendered, and the successful practicing of it have increased, but a supreme contempt for mankind?" The very striking ending to the story,

> "Yes," the sheriff said. "The Book itself says somewhere, *Know thyself.* Ain't there another book somewhere that says, *Man, fear thyself, thine arrogance and vanity and pride?* You ought to know; you claim to be a book man. Didn't you tell me that's what the luckcharm on your watch chain means? What book is that in?"
> "It's in all of them," Uncle Gavin said. "The good ones, I mean. It's said in a lot of different ways, but it's there." (p. 131)

might indeed be the reason why so many critics wish to read "An Error in Chemistry" as a chapter in the development of Gavin Stevens. But the heart of the story concerns themes wider than one character, however major he may be in other novels.

"Knight's Gambit," longest of the stories in the collection to which it gives its name, is also the richest presentation of the community-outlander themes. Gavin Stevens and Chick Mallison, as described by a third person narrator,[10] are present, and partake of the themes in an even more personal manner than before. The prime actors, however, are the members of the Harriss family. The two children begin the story by interrupting Stevens at his chess game. Their alienation from the community is made explicit in the very description of themselves and their circumstances:

> Their name was Harriss. They were brother and sister. At first glance they might have been twins, not just to strangers but to most of Jefferson too. Because there were probably not half a dozen people in Yoknapatawpha County who actually knew which one was the oldest. They lived six miles from town on what twenty years ago had been just another plantation raising cotton for the market and corn and hay to feed the mules which made the cotton. But now it was a county (or for that matter, a north Mississippi) landmark: a mile square of white panel and rail paddock and pasture fences and electric-lit stables and a once-simple country house transmogrified now into something a little smaller than a Before-the-War Hollywood set. (p. 135)

Their mother, Melisandre Backus, of an old Jefferson family, had married a "stranger not only to Jefferson but to all north Mississippi and perhaps to all the rest of Mississippi too as far as anyone knew," and

for the next five years what his uncle called the whole broad generation of spinster aunts who, still alive seventy-five years after the Civil War, are the backbone of the South's social and political economic solidarity too, watched it as you watch the unfolding story in the magazine installments. (pp. 148–49)

Thus the community observes as another outlander, like Anse Holland and Joel Flint, moves in and appropriates to himself the community's wealth, for after only a year "the grandfather was dead and that Christmas Harriss took command of the plantation." The people look on:

And now not only Jefferson but the whole country watched it, not only . . . the spinster aunts . . . but the men too, and not just men from the town who had only six miles to go, but farmers who had the whole county to cross.

They would come by whole families in battered dusty cars and wagons, or singly on horses or mules taken last night from the plow, to stop along the road and watch gangs of strange men with enough machinery to have built a highway or a reservoir, disc and terrace the old fields once dedicated to simple profit-producing corn and cotton, and sow them to pasture grass costing more per pound than sugar.

They would ride past mile after mile of white-painted panel fence, to sit in the cars and wagons or on the horses and mules, and watch long rows of stables being built of better material than was in most of their houses, with electric lights and illuminated clocks and running water and screened windows and such as most of their homes didn't have. . . . (p. 154)

The theme of the outlander coming into the community, and the variation of alienation within that community, are joined together in the Harriss situation. The husband, commuting by "private aeroplane" to New Orleans, after finishing the stables turns to rebuilding the house:

That is, the new house was going to occupy the same ground the old one would have covered if there had been four of them just alike nailed together. It had been just a house, of one story, with the gallery across the front where the old master would sit in his home-made chair with his toddy and his Catullus; when Harriss got through with it, it looked like the Southern mansion in the moving picture, only about five times as big and ten times as Southern. (p. 155)

Harriss' act of intrusion and usurpation is complicated not only by the fact that his ostentation alienates himself and his family from the community, but that the very method of his display is a hyperbolic extension of the modes of the community itself—"ten times" is the factor the community observer arrives at.

"Strange outlanders" come to visit Harriss, "driving big shining sports cars fast through town and fast along the road which was just a country road . . . no matter what he had built at one end of it," and, like a feudal baron, Harriss provides for the inevitable hit-and-run accidents by supplying "a mass of coins and banknotes and a few . . . checks signed in blank, in a canvas sack hanging from the inside knob of the front door, the farmer or his wife or his child riding up to the front door and saying 'hog' or 'mule' or 'hen.' " The Harriss family "had become a secondary source of rural income for that whole six miles of road like the gathering and selling of blackberries or eggs."

Melisandre Backus Harriss, however, is kept at a distance from all of this. She and the children travel in Europe. But neither does she become a member of the European community or even the travel elite, for the cards she writes to her girlhood friends "would be postmarked from Rome or London or Paris or Vienna or Cairo, but they hadn't been bought there." Instead, Melisandre uses old notecards from home, "oldtimey cards out of the old time, giving off the faint whisper of old sentiment and old thought impervious to the foreign names and addresses, as if she had carried them across the ocean with her from a bureau drawer in the old house which these five and ten years had no longer existed." She had traveled among "the crowned heads of Europe," but "without ever really knowing she had left Yoknapatawpha County." After Harriss dies, she returns to the house unchanged, like "a breath say of sachet, as if one of the old bureau drawers or such from the old house had remained stubborn and constant against all change and alteration, not only impervious but not even aware that it had resisted change, inside the parvenue's monstrous mushroom." She is kept safely as a member of the community, and it is something else which disturbs even beyond Harriss' death: "it was not she which was the ghost; the wraith was Harriss' monstrous house."

What brings the Harriss children to Gavin Stevens is a further complication and enrichment of the outlander theme. Captain Sebastian Gauldres, an Argentine cavalry officer, is a house guest of Mrs. Harriss, and the children, outsiders themselves, resent this international outlander. "I don't intend that a fortune-hunting Spick shall marry my mother," says Max Harriss. "A unicorn" is Stevens' term for the new outsider, but his challenge to the integrity of the family is a more substantial one than merely the fact of his foreign heritage. The Harriss girl tells Stevens of the rivalry between the Captain and her brother Max.

Stevens fulfills his detective role by anticipating the murder of Gauldres and by, in dramatic form, preventing it. Otherwise, he is characterized in this story by his passivity. The narrator several times observes that Stevens would be clarifying events for his nephew, except that "this was the year during which his uncle seemed to have stopped talking very much about anything"; Stevens' whole mood is one of "taciturnity." What, then, is Stevens' relationship to the larger themes of the story?

Stevens' participation in the theme of community is actually the greatest in this last of the *Knight's Gambit* stories. His marriage to Melisandre at the end is, of course, his most personal act in the volume, and it squares with the story's larger theme, for by taking her back into the community Stevens completes the full circle of her adventures. But of even larger thematic import is the way the other end of the plot is tied up, partially through the office of Gavin Stevens. The entry of Sebastian Gauldres has widened the scope of the community; he is an outlander not just to Jefferson, nor northern Mississippi, or even the South, but to the entire United States. And the most important event to the national community at the time of the story, the Second World War, figures in the resolution of nearly all of the characters. The reader has been constantly reminded of the social time during which the various events of the story have taken place. Harriss makes his fortune as a bootlegger (Prohibition), diversifies into newer markets (repeal), and is shot by a rival gangster during "what was going to be the first year of the new war in Europe," 1939.

The first years of the European conflict are depicted within the American community by Chick's participation in ROTC, and especially by his fears of being left out of the battle. He ardently wishes not to be an outsider to this event. But military service is treated in its full complexity. When Stevens uncovers Max's plot, he gives the boy the alternatives, "Enlist or else." The reader should recall that, from the start, Stevens, as a member of the local draft board, has been concerned that Max has never registered—one more aspect of his family's alienation from the community. Now, however, the boy, like his mother, returns. The action of the story ends on a Saturday; "The next day was December seventh." Gauldres, last of the characters left uninvolved, marries the young Harriss girl and enlists in the United States army as a private. Thus, on two levels, *he* is taken into the community, and the story concludes.

"Knight's Gambit," then, is a story of outsiders and communities, and Gavin Stevens has a part to play within these larger themes. To read it as simply a Gavin Stevens story is to overestimate one character, while reviewing the action with an eye to the major theme makes Stevens and everyone else in the story more important. On this higher level, the story succeeds.

The community-outlander theme is the heart and strength of the *Knight's Gambit* collection. In all of the stories it figures prominently, and each story becomes more technically perfect and artistically powerful as it centers more directly on that theme. The strictly ratiocinative sections diminish as we read through Faulkner's efforts of the late twenties and early thirties into the products of his more mature years; Gavin Stevens, the agent of this ratocination, becomes at the same time more organic to the action, until in the final story all elements work harmoniously. The six stories, grouped together, present a rich exploration of that theme as it passes through its various configurations: outsider from without the community, outsider from within. Again, the title story itself most perfectly melds the two variations into one community tale.

Communities and outsiders run through the greatest of Faulkner's work (as opposed to the figure of Gavin Stevens, who plays his major role in novels written past the period of Faulkner's major achievement). One thinks of Joanna Burden, Lena Grove, and Joe Christmas, in *Light in August;*[11] Thomas Sutpen himself and then Charles Bon in *Absalom, Absalom!;*[12] and the community and Flem Snopes in *The Hamlet*. On a more intimate basis, one might compare Monk with Mink Snopes, Jackson Fentry with Byron Bunch, and make the rich comparison of Harriss with Sutpen. But to do this would lead to, perhaps, the same problems that two decades of Gavin Stevens comparisons have given us. *Knight's Gambit* is a separate book, consisting of some inferior pieces, but together signalling the "form and integration" that Faulkner demanded of all short story collections, no less his own.

Willard Motley: Making and Unmaking
of *Knock on Any Door*

WILLARD MOTLEY (1909–65) desperately wanted to be a major writer, but circumstances conspired against him. Accidents of birth, economics, and publishing history combined to define him as a minor exponent of an obsolete realism. As a black author dealing almost exclusively with white characters and as a proletarian novelist in boom times, Motley became a natural candidate for anyone's hostilities toward or frustrations with the earlier age.[1] He became a candidate for those furies because his *Knock on Any Door* was a runaway best-seller almost as soon as it was published in 1947. It was so successful that in 1949 it was made into a motion picture starring Humphrey Bogart, and introducing John Derek in the role of Nick Romano. That is the way *Knock on Any Door* is remembered today: as a popular success, not a serious novel. There is only half a paragraph on Motley and his book in the major literary history of the period, and in it his achievement is dismissed. "It is not fair to say that this kind of novel reveals the bankruptcy of naturalism, but since Motley invents no new thing and casts no new light, one must conclude that naturalism is in serious trouble."[2]

Perhaps. The trouble with the judgment is that it is based on limited knowledge that leads—understandably, but unfortunately—to a conclusion that Motley set out to adapt worn-out formulas so that he could produce a potboiler. That is in complete opposition to the truth. Six years after he died, two major accumulations of Motley's papers were discovered: eight file cartons at the University of Wisconsin, and nearly one hundred cubic feet of additional material moldering in a basement on Chicago's South Side.[3] In addition to scores of published and unpublished manuscripts, an extensive set of diaries, and hundreds of letters to

Reprinted by permission from Jerome Klinkowitz and Karen Wood, *Proof* 3, copyright 1973, Joseph Katz, Columbia, S.C.

and from literary celebrities, Motley had retained the full correspondence regarding publication of *Knock on Any Door.* They make possible his redemption, because those letters document the novel's making—a quarter-century story of a writer who, beginning with a children's column for the *Chicago Defender,* abandoned his middle-class heritage to seek the lower depths of life—and also its unmaking. For what can be traced in those letters and verified in surviving manuscripts of the novel is that *Knock on Any Door* was written as a bold, experimental novel that was turned into a commercial property as it passed through the hands of several publishers.

During the thirties, Motley tramped the United States as a hobo, collecting episodes for his diaries and rewriting some into a book-length manuscript entitled "Adventure," fragments of which were published in travel magazines of the period. In 1939, "when a late arrival after Richard Wright and Nelson Algren" to the Works Project Administration (WPA) Writer's Project, Motley met the proletarian novelist Jack Conroy. "He was the first 'professional' to encourage me when I got up enough nerve to show him a chapter of in-progress KNOCK ON ANY DOOR."[4] Two years earlier, the young slum writer had been offered payment in fishing tackle and hunting gear for one of his stories;[5] once introduced to proletarian literary society in Chicago, he was given a series of Newberry Library and Julius Rosenwald fellowships which let him complete two novels. One was entitled *Leave Without Illusions.* Over a dozen major publishers rejected it because of its frank content before the Macmillan Company bought in in 1945.[6] That firm then developed grave reservations about the economics involved in publishing the book, in part because it was so long. Judging from typescripts surviving in Motley's papers, the original work was over 2,000 pages—a million words. After cutting, rewriting, and retitling, *Leave Without Illusions* finally was published by another firm, Appleton-Century. Now, however, it was *Knock on Any Door.*

Knock on Any Door was not what Motley had written. Many of the complaints lodged against it today are more properly attributable to publishing conditions in the late 1940s. On November 9, 1945, the editor-in-chief of Macmillan, Harold S. Latham, wrote Motley that he would like to publish "Leave Without Illusions," the massive document which after so many rejections had found its way to his Fifth Avenue offices. But Latham wanted some revisions, which were to be made in collaboration with a free-lance editor Macmillan had hired for the occasion. Two days

later Theodore M. Purdy wrote Motley in private, introducing himself as
the editor and making clear what was between the lines of Latham's letter. At issue were Macmillan's fears for their reputation. "I think they
are still smarting under the reviews—though not the sales—of 'Forever
Amber,' " Purdy surmised. He also made several off-the-record comments, which he placed on the record twenty-five years later at a symposium of the PEN American Center: Macmillan's executives, he
reported, feared police censorship, but also "were worried that the un-
flattering picture of Chicago life given by the book might lead to resent-
ment on the part of the school boards and other purchasers of Macmillan
books in Chicago and the west, and that business might suffer as a
result."[7] Although Macmillan wanted the book "desexed" and its location changed to an anonymous American city, Purdy promised Motley
that honesty in both areas could remain. In his paper, Purdy recalled the
changes he did make:

The principal problems were Will's tendency to introduce too many secondary
characters and incidents, and to get away from Nick and his story; too much and
too long dialogue (Will always tended to reproduce talk accurately but unselec-
tively); possible libel, since he named real people and places in the original version of the book; and toning down the language and the sex scenes, which now
seem tame but then worried many who read the manuscript.

Macmillan brought Motley to New York in December 1945, where
with Purdy he worked on revisions through the following March. "The
Fall of a Sparrow," as the novel was then titled, was ready for produc-
tion in April; but the transfer of one Macmillan editor and the death of
another placed it in jeopardy. Purdy cautioned against further revisions.[8]
When he found a job with Appleton-Century the next month, he took
the manuscript with him. Samuel Rapport, manager of trade books, for-
mally requested Motley's submission on 21 June 1946, and less than two
weeks later, on 2 July, he telegraphed the firm's commitment to publish.
Yet because of several peculiar features in it, problems with the
manuscript began almost at once. Permissions fees for the many songs
Motley wanted quoted could not possibly be financed; nearly at all the
italicized passages of poetic prose (similar to those beginning and ending
the book's published version) would have to be cut; and the simple difficulty of manufacturing such a large and complex novel would require
the writer to accept smaller royalties. Motley accepted the terms, but not
without lingering complaint, set forth in his November 29, 1946 letter to
Rapport:

Since this is my first book I am in no position to ask special consideration in regard to royalty terms. However, as a matter of principle I think that I should tell you now that I do not feel that straight ten per cent agreements of this sort are fair to an author. This is, after all, a terrific cut from the fifteen per cent royalty agreement after 25,000 copies have been sold, the twelve percent royalty agreement after 12,500 copies have been sold. I do realize your problem in cost and manufacture but had assumed that if we could cut the book sufficiently and in this manner brought it down to a three dollar price that my royalty terms would remain as fixed in our agreement. After talking to Ted I signed cheerfully if somewhat disappointedly as perhaps would not have been the case had I had an agent. Certainly there should be some increased remuneration if a book becomes established and becomes a success, and obviously the costs to the publisher must decline to some extent as additional editions are printed. If the book really goes over big I am wondering if some sort of adjustment cannot be made later on.

If in the future you should publish other books of mine, I would of course expect a sliding scale of royalties, and I want to make it clear that in signing the enclosed letter of agreement to accept a ten per cent royalty on THE FALL OF A SPARROW, I do not in any way commit myself to similar terms on future books.

I hope that with the decreased royalty it may be possible for you to do some special advertising and promotion when my book appears next spring. I will talk this over with Ted and hope I'll have a chance to talk to you and Mr. Bueno about it before the book comes out.

I hope that you will not think that I don't appreciate your enthusiasm and backing of my book. I do very much and have enjoyed working with you and Ted on it.[9]

In reply, Motley was told that Appleton-Century would make a minimum first printing of 25,000 copies; that at least $10,000 would be budgeted for promotion, much more than for any previous first novel; and that subsequent printings, because of their smaller size, were no cheaper than the first.[10] In the meantime, Purdy had flown to Chicago and helped Motley further reduce the manuscript (down to 843 pages—250,000 words—by 26 August) in the hope of helping him win better royalty terms.[11] The attempt failed. The novel continued to change, however, even while it was in press, going through many re-titlings before it appeared as *Knock on Any Door* at the head of Appleton-Century's spring 1947 list. Reviews were generally favorable and sales were strong (300,000 copies were sold in 1947-48), but the novel was not the one Motley had written.

The manuscript he had written and tried to sell as "Leave Without Illusions" is so radically different from the book published as *Knock on*

Any Door that collation between the two is practically impossible. Someday the original should be published; now, however, insight into it can begin with the first 1,000 words to be cut—Motley's unpublished preface to his novel. It reveals his intentions in the book, which were obscured and then suppressed during the interminable stages of cutting.

PREFACE

I.

I don't know whether this is a "good" book or a "bad" book. I don't know whether this is a realistic book or a sentimental book in a wrapping of "hard-boiled" writing, an "obscene" book or an "artistic" book—whatever "artistic" means. And I don't know how to write a book. All I knew was what I wanted to say. And tried to say it. All I know is that this is an honest book.

First, I wanted to tell the truth about Nick and the world Nick lived in. Second, I feel that in writing the author is of minor importance and should be a lay-figure in the hands of his characters rather than the other way around; that the author doesn't belong on a pedestal looking down at his characters—however sympathetically. I feel that the author's style, his language, his idiom, should be that of his characters in any large and seriously-undertaken portrayal in which a whole environment is treated with a single character as the pivot around which his story turns—that of necessity he must see through the eyes of his main character; that in so doing he has a much better chance of bringing the character and the story to life. Some writers write at a great distance from their characters; some very close to them. I wanted to write as a part of the leading character. Why? So as to make him as real as possible; to try to make the reader know him and understand him, know why Nick was Nick. Okay. Nick was important—I wasn't. Style, grammar, sentences fitting neatly into the four walls of syntax, subtle inference instead of the direct fact, pleasant and artificial words instead of the short and ugly ones weren't important. Nick, and how he felt, thought, saw, smelled, talked, looked, were all that was important. I had to get as close to Nick as I could, think, see, feel as he did. Narrate through his eyes whenever possible. That is what I have tried to do.

II.

Of course "Nick" and "Emma" are living people. I make no pretensions at having created them. "Nick," in reality, is two youths I know and my conception of a third. Nick's experiences in this book start with the experiences of the other two Nicks. They are still boys being shaped by an environment and "reformative" system with which this book deals. It is my hope that what happens to Nick Romano, and what could happen to them, won't. "Emma" is a woman of my acquaintance, now forty-eight years old. She has been very generous in giving me the details of her early life which I have "dressed down" or "dressed up" to suit my purposes. It is only from the time that she is eighteen that fact and fiction take separate courses.

Both "Nick" and "Emma" knew that they were being written about and have given me permission to live their lives for them on these pages. Practically all of the other characters are friends and acquaintances of mine. Most of Nick's experiences throughout this book are true happenings. Most of the incidents have happened. Most of them are happening over and over again, in this environment and in all environments like it all over the world. As much as many writers like to take upon themselves the "divinity" of having written a book I can but humbly say that this is not mine but a project between me and the people I have met and known. And I must add that what I saw of them, what was acted out before my eyes on Halsted Street, Maxwell Street, West Madison Street; on relief benches and WPA projects; in reform schools and courtrooms; on street corners and in taverns—and most of all how these people looked is beyond any words of mine. What they said, the way they said it, the way their eyes and faces moved in talking, the way they told about themselves is beyond the words of any written language.

Let's get this straight. This is a true story. The plot is mine. Nothing else. This is the interweaving of real incidents and living people into a fictional whole. This touches, in one way or another, the manner in which a third of a nation and no doubt a half of the world is forced to live. These statements I make, and wish to emphasize, because of the second of two types of readers. There is the type of reader who knows that the things in serious novels come directly from life. Then there is a second class of readers. This type of reader closes every novel, no matter how serious, with the opinion that it is "just fiction." Again, and again, this is not "just fiction."

III.

Every honest writer has, one time or another, asked himself: "Why do I write? Of what use is the writer to society? Isn't he, too, just a parasite?" He has been dissatisfied with the complacent and stock answer of beauty for beauty's sake and his contribution to culture. He has come out of his ivory tower and lives, now, like ordinary human beings. His descent hasn't been completely a self-exile. Economics have played a part. The writer is no longer maintained by kings, emperors, wealthy groups of patrons whom he must flatter. He has to earn his living extraneous to his writing and on an 8-hour a day job, or, until recently, on a government writers' project.

And the question has persisted: "Why do I write?"

The writer of today is a serious young man writing between two wars valleyed by a depression. He is, himself, of the middle, lower-middle and poor classes. He has, if not actually experienced, seen all around him the wrongs, injustices and inequalities of the world. He has seen power and money as criteria of success where he once wrote of "godliness" and humility. He has seen hate and lust and prejudice and ignorance triumphant where once he wrote of honesty and virtue and love as being always triumphant. And most acutely of all he has seen all of these things used as a larger and larger club on the people the poorer the people got.

And he has asked himself: "Why do I write?"

Before a writer is a writer he is a man. His material is the other men and women in the world. It seems to me that the writer today, since the advent of Freud, science, the machine which uses him, too, like a rubber stamp, wars and depressions, the retreat from God, destruction of the ivory tower, political and economic trends, has turned more and more to his fellow man for the answer to their problems and his own. The writer, today, sees himself in these other people and these men and women in him. And if he is honest, first as a man and secondly as a writer, he cannot but write about them and against the things that oppress and injure his fellow man. In other words the writer approaches his subject matter—his fellow man—in humility and understanding, in sympathy and identification—but without glorification. And he tries—only the serious writer knows how hard—to tell the truth, frankly and unshrinkingly.

The writer who attempts to apply his abilities seriously of necessity goes to life. Life is the things that are closest around him, to him in his environment of experiences and acquaintances; the things that call most profoundly for his attention or have been most deeply thrust upon it. The writer would like to say that all's well with the world. He can't. He is, of course, no different than anyone else (try as he sometimes does to be different), except in sensitivity, if in that. In his attempt to transpose his emotions to others he finds, not infrequently, that he hasn't a very pleasant story to tell. Therefore he very often feels that his function, as a responsible citizen and another of many men in the world, is to show, in a wrapping of fiction, just what's wrong with the world and where some of the faults lie. Perhaps in his assumed garments of "tough guy" he is a moralist, a reformer, or even a disappointed romanticist. Nevertheless he is today writing more honestly than ever before. He hasn't had to reach out to the working man, the underdog, the prostitute, the criminal—he has found himself one with them; their problems and defeats his. He writes in a world he didn't make but he isn't, in his writing, making a world of his own, a place of "pure beauty" or art and entirely untrue to life as he and his fellow men know it. He is, instead, tearing down the world as it is and feels that although the pen may not be mightier than the sword each novel against a world as it is is the tearing away of one more brick of the phoney structure and that in this way he is helping in the making of a new world. If this type of writing is propaganda then the modern writer is a propagandist; if this be "inartistic" then art, "pure art" has always been a parasitic growth scratching at the surface of life and reality and receiving board and keep from patrons whom it was desireable to please and flatter in exchange for the delight of being a fat and self-pleased parasite in an ivory tower. However if this is propaganda I'm not too sure then that everything that has ever been written isn't propaganda of one sort or another. What did they write? What about the great masters? What did they write? What did they paint? For whom? What was Da Vinci propagandizing? And the Victorians? And our present day slick-pulp-movie writers?

IV

The chief complaint against realistic writing is that it is unpleasant. It isn't realism that is unpleasant but life. And writing will become more "beautiful" as life becomes more beautiful for all people, and at about the same pace. People, turning quickly to an "escape" novel or rushing in to a movie say that realistic writing "depresses them"; that life is bad enough without having to read about it; that they are looking for beauty and "some pleasure out of life." People are afraid, in print, of the real words for things—words that are definitely in their vocabulary, and knowledge of which they have at least a glimmering. We have too long been a nation of adolescents. The reading public has been too easily lead [*sic*] away from life, has too often escaped living and understanding and sympathy and *constructive rebuilding* by route of the mass of literature written today. The public, even while being pleased and lulled and flattered by self-identity with handsome-and-successful hero or beautiful-and-perfectly-limbed heroine, has known the unreality of what is written; has gone past the gates of the carnival and up on the sweetly spinning ferris wheel while the organ piped on the merry-go-round, fully conscious that within the carnival grounds is nothing as it is in life. But it's fun to go to the carnival, to go to the circus, to the movies, to see the fat ladies, to see the grinning clowns, and the lady sawed in half, and the nigger dodger, and the pink pop and cotton candy. Inside the carnival grounds there is escape from thinking. Escape from social consciousness. Escape from self-identity with the poor, the wretched, the puzzled, the humble children in the marketplace.

V.

Meanwhile the serious writers put the pavement and the cobblestones and the sweat and blood and tears of real people on paper. The serious writers tear the stories from them like terrible tumors they must rip out of their chests and the general public either makes a best seller of *The Robe* or writes off the serious novel as "just fiction." Thus the Tom Joads, the Bigger Thomases, the Studs Lonigans, the Bruno Biceks live and suffer and die on paper and the young men writing today bring more life-and-blood characters to tear another brick, and another, and another from the structure of a phoney and unjust world in order to build a new world.

VI.

Again, Nick Romano is not "just fiction." I knew two of him in their formative periods. I know at least twenty of him who live within a mile from where this is written. Even now, looking out the window I can see Leavitt's and the hot dog stand with a friend of mine, a young fellow who can very easily become a Nick Romano, buying a hot dog.

And again, I don't know whether this is a "good" book or a "bad" book. One friend, reading part of it, said that it was an ugly story. Good! Nick lived an ugly life. If the story is ugly, if it leaves the reader with the impression I attempted to get across—with sympathy for and understanding of Nick and knowledge that it is about the reader as much as it is about Nick then I have not failed. Nothing is exaggerated. The conduct on streets, in places and neighborhoods named is the conduct of those streets, places, neighborhoods. The whole attempt has been to give an exact and undistorted picture in its entirety of the environment and the places named in this book. My advice to anyone who, after finishing the book, believes that I have exaggerated, is to go down to West Madison Street, Halsted Street, Maxwell Street—or into a courtroom and find out for himself. An old writer-friend once told me that once a man starts writing he starts posing. I have tried to avoid posing of any kind, even as the "tough guy." Where I have gone out-of-bounds it was only in my anxiety in bringing you the story of this, my neighborhood. This is as truthfully as I can tell the story, and perhaps as anyone could. My only recommendation is that it is an honest book.

WILLARD MOTLEY
"Nick's neighborhood"
1943[12]

At any rate, the novel was published and was doing well. Motley was pleased by its commercial success, but he had not stopped thinking of it as a serious book too, even though by now it was only a shadow of what he had written. When Charles Lee gave *Knock on Any Door* a favorable review in the *New York Times,* tempering his approval with a few reservations about the book's originality, Motley rushed to its defense in a letter to Purdy. The terms of the defense, and the passion with which they are expressed, show that after four years of literary surgery on his novel, his original attitude toward it had not changed.

Goddamn it, Ted, I'm sore! I've just finished Charles Lee's review of my book and I don't like it at all. If he had said that he didn't like the book and thought people shouldn't waste their money on it that would have been all right. I could understand that and approve of it as an honest opinion. But his praise and blame, straddling the fence attitude and implications were damn indecent. I started to write to him and say so but thought that in the heat of the moment that would perhaps not be the best thing to do. Instead I am writing to you. You may pass this letter on to him if you wish or use all or any of it for my publicity purposes that you choose. Here goes—
I have perhaps read less than any author who has had a book published in the last ten years or more. Of the present day writers I've read some Steinbeck, some Dos Passos and one of Cain's novels. No Caldwell. Unfortunately I came from a lower middle-class background where movies took the place of books and for a good part of my young manhood I spent much of my time in athletics. In fact until I moved to the slums and started going to Hull-House I didn't know that Farrell or Dreiser existed (despite high school English classes), this being at a time after I started the novel. I haven't read Studs Lonigan and when I was working on the book refused to read it because I was afraid that his style might influence me. In fact the only thing I've read by Farrell is his collection of short stories, and quite recently. I haven't read "Native Son." Again I was afraid of subconscious influence. I didn't read "Never Come Morning" until after I'd finished my book for the same reason. When I had finished my book and sent it off then I read Dreiser's "An American Tragedy." I think it is a great book. Whenever his book and mine are compared I feel humble as hell and as if I am taking part in some sort of a fraud. Also when it came to revision and it was decided that we would end the book with a scenic of the neighborhood and the line "Nick? Knock on any door down this street." I at first rejected the idea, fearing the readers might think that I was copying after Dreiser.

Concerning Mr. Lee: There are some reviewers who have the lazy habit of grouping writers in schools with a "master." He could have found out just how much of Dreiser and Farrell I had read. In fact he could have learned my ignorance of most of what has been written and could have compared my book to Dreiser and Farrell without such quotes as "the over-sedulousness of Mr. Motley's apings . . . the Farrell-like accent on verbal shock." In other words, he could have reviewed the book fairly and on its own feet. He might even have learned further that writers who attack problems of society perhaps write somewhat alike because they go to life for their problems, live in the mess, and react angrily, honestly, sincerely.

Also, during the writing of the book I often asked Drews and Sandy, who were reading it: "This isn't like Farrell is it? This doesn't sound like Dreiser does it? I'm not doing over again what Wright did, am I? What Algren did, am I?"

Mr. Lee further speaks of a "sordid sequence," of suicides, or murders. Mrs. Roosevelt wasn't particularly shocked. She ends her article by saying "I hope that this book will stir many people to action in their own communities." Also if Mr. Lee had read the book a little more carefully he would have discovered that there is but one suicide and one murder in it.

Mr. Lee seems to think that psychiatry and Freud should have been dragged into the book. I wasn't writing this type of novel here. And the psychological factors are, are they not, inherent in the story and in Nick? Horace Cayton, in his review (for the New Republic) seems to think so . . . "Showing more insight than those who glorify or damn gangsters, Motley has exposed to view, and in a most subtle way, the essential passivity of the killer. He has shown that the real motivation is fear. He has demonstrated that it is not by accident that there is such a high rate of homosexuality among these frightened personalities. The protagonist of Motley's book, the Chicago gangsters of the 20s, and the Hitler Legions of the 30s have characteristics in common—the compulsion to rush into danger in an attempt to conquer anxiety arising out of their fear or their own passivity. If the book says anything it says, "Frighten people and you either make abject creatures or killers of them . . . Motley has indeed stated the psychological problem arising out of the economic and social conflicts which face America and the world."

Finally any time that Mr. Lee is in Chicago I'll be glad to take him on an escorted tour of the city. I would ask him to wear old clothes with me and for two or three days hang down on West Madison with me, around Maxwell Street, Halsted Street. We would then change into very good clothes and hang in the better neighborhoods for five or ten minutes. He might then learn why so many of our criminals come from the slums and so few from good neighborhoods. And in a few days along West Madison Street he would of a certainty learn that my novel is not "distorted to fit a thesis." I would also introduce him to the young men in particular who live in the slums. I would take him to their homes, introduce him to their parents, and he would also learn why some men of the slums "turn out to be socially useful citizens."

Come along, Mr. Lee![13]

Earlier, in a letter to Purdy on the eve of *Knock on Any Door*'s publication Motley had talked of future work. After sharing excitement over good advance comments and forthcoming movie rights, he continued:

And now about my second book. I am, of course, anxious to do it and am unhappy when I am not writing. I surely hope to have it ready for publication in the spring of 1948. If it isn't ready by then do you know whether or not A-C would be interested in a book of short stories, a Skid Row book, with some of my photographs included (if that is practical)? The novel could then make the fall of 1948. Appleton-Century has spent a lot of money and will continue to do so to advertise and sell KNOCK ON ANY DOOR. After reading the first book the market that A-C has built up for me will expect much of the same type of writing in the second book—action, suspense, drama. I will at that time owe a lot to my publishers for having built me up and it is only natural that they should want a book with the elements that sold the first book. The Nick story—the material—had these elements inherent in it. Unfortunately the book I am working on, OF NIGHT, hasn't this kind of drama. But it is a book I must do. If not as a second, then as a third book. If not as a third, then as a fourth. It is a book I know I can do and make come alive. As it stands it needs a lot of rewriting and a lot of it should be junked. However I still feel that it is a big subject and a good subject. On the strength of the outline for it I won both Newberry (Rockerfeller) [sic]and Rosenwald fellowships. Also I still feel that the Dave story is an integral part of that book. The whole subject grips my imagination and calls to me (damn it, I hope I don't sound arty!)

If, at this time—the world being in the shape it is these days—the overall subject matter of the book is unpopular then perhaps it shouldn't be done now. On the other hand—again the world being as it is—I'd feel dishonest if I didn't, somehow, in my writing touch on some of the big problems.

Now the question comes up: would A-C consider the third book as a follow-up to KNOCK ON ANY DOOR? This third book is in reality a sequel to the second one though the main characters are not the main characters of the second book. This third book, WE FISHED ALL NIGHT, I have already briefly discussed with you. Three fellows back from the war. One, a poet, cracks up mentally. Two, a minor labor leader, comes back morally wrecked. Three, a young fellow from a bad background comes back physically wrecked, having lost a leg in the war. He is at first a liberal, then poses as a liberal, runs for a political office (some of the big boys getting behind him because they feel that they can use him for their own interests) on the strength of his service in the war and his loss of a limb for America. He loses the election, joins the American Legion, becomes a reactionary and successful. Meanwhile the poet shuts off more and more of his friends, breaks with the girl who loves him and has waited for him, becomes paranoiac, sits alone in cheap cafeterias scribbling gibberish on the edges of newspapers. Afraid of people he fears showing any of his writing to anyone, stuffs his scribblings into his pockets. Meanwhile the labor leader, as a hang-over from Paris, has become interested in women other than his wife and his desires scale down until he is interested in teen-aged school girls and—at least mentally—is prepared for rape. On the verge of attacking a young girl he instead goes to a meeting where there is labor strife and is killed. Spotted into the main story would be short sections—sort of portraits—of other returned veterans, their attitudes and reactions, their post-war patterns.

This isn't a positive book. It is, I suppose, an anti-war book, with war the protagonist (villain). It would be a book easy to write once I have it well outlined, would run only about 350 pages and would, I think, take only four or five months to write.

Thinking about writing this story I have an immediate conflict. I don't want to do labor a disservice. Would such a novel be injurious?

I have ideas for other novels kicking around in my head but none of which I can get worked up about at the present time with books two and three staring me in the face. I'll set down, loosely, some of these ideas.

I would, of course, like at some later date to do a book somewhat similar to the Nick story but with a girl from an orphanage as the main character; a sort of counter-part for Nick. And I'd like to do the kind of novel you suggested—a family—and over three generations. This book I'd like to base somewhat on my mother's life and make it a book about Negroes, not as such, but as Negroes integrating themselves into the life of a big city (Chicago) or cracking up under the social and economic pressures. The main theme would be (1) a young southern Catholic Negro girl in a small town near New Orleans. Her childhood, early youth, the town life, the village priest (an old Frenchman) and his opposition to southern attitudes about Negroes. The girl marries, moves north to Chicago, goes to night school, bears a son and a daughter (2) the lives of the son and daughter (based somewhat on my brother and sister) concurrently with the life of the mother (3) the lives of the grandchildren—some stabilizing themselves, some going to pieces.

Again, this material hasn't gripped me yet but I intend going out to my mother's once a week while working on my second book and taking notes on her life.

Another novel I'd like to do is one on old people who have reared their families but are now of no further use and are stuck into old folks homes. Again not nearly enough material on hand as yet.

Another idea is a novel in three sections around the "three sides of a circle" idea. (Section One) A boy aged twelve thinks his grandparents are his parents. His life as a kid. His younger sister. The people who come to visit (among them a married sister, a man who infrequently comes to the house and who turns out to be his father). When the boy is 12 he misbehaves and his grandmother in a fit of anger tells him he isn't her son, that the woman he thinks is his sister is really his mother. His reaction to all of them. He later learns that his little sister is a second child by his mother. The little sister is never told and he resents what he feels is unfair treatment. The little sister dies. (Section Two) The boy now about 18. His grandmother's story of it. How his mother was only 14 and his father a man of 36, living in the house, meeting the child on her way from school. That the man was taken into the house to live when the grandfather contacted syphilis from some woman and is in the hospital for months. How this man was taken in as a roomer to help meet household expenses. The shame to the family and the marriage to this man to save the boy from being a bastard. How his mother was sent to stay with a doctor friend of the family and worked for him until the child came. How the marriage was annulled and the grandparents took the boy to rear as their own. How only the oldest residents in the neighborhood knew the truth. How his father had secretly met the girl, his mother, and how his little sister had been the bastard child of that second intimacy. (Section Three) The boy, now about 21, and his mother's story of the affair—how his father, when living in the house had been his grandmother's boyfriend (at the time the grandfather was in the hospital). How the grandmother had forced her, after the second child, to marry a man she didn't love but who would make a good husband and provider. How the grandparents took the second child and raised it too while the mother and husband had children of their own. The mother tells the story vindictively, with a subconscious feeling of rivalry toward her mother and a hatred of her mother as if now trying to get even by turning the boy against his grandmother.

The boy, who has grown very close to the grandmother, resents the mother, sees the grandmother as a young woman, not as an old lady as she now is, but a young woman needing sex, her husband in the hospital with syphilis, and understands the relationship, if it is true—the truth of which he isn't sure. (ends on this note with the boy feeling even closer to his grandmother)

And finally, Ted, I have several hundred notes to work into a novel about young middle class kids (ages 16 to 23) who break with their families and try to live the life of bohemians on Chicago's Near North Side but who end by becoming delinquents of a type different from Nick. As yet I have no plot for this material which, despite its humor of situation and dialogue, has a tragic undertone and would have to have a tragic end for at least one of its main characters.

So you see I have a lot of stuff to work with but only a couple of things that really grab hold of me at this moment. I started out to write a letter and have ended by writing a baby manuscript. I hope you will forgive me for burdening you with so much reading and that you will let me know just what you think.[14]

Although he eventually wrote it all and stored it with his papers, Willard Motley did not publish one-tenth the work he described to Purdy. The next year his adaptation of *Knock on Any Door* won a $50,000 screenwriting contest but had to be withdrawn because of Breen Office censorship; the second novel, *We Fished All Night* (1951), was massively reshaped before publication; and *Let No Man Write My Epitaph* (1958) was a sequel to *Knock on Any Door* both in theme and in publishing history. The last decade of his life was spent in Mexico, a frustrating period for himself and his agents of revisions and rejections. His themes—racial assimilation, sexual adventure, human pity—were reshaped to fit existing stereotypes, whether of postwar timidity or, in the case of the posthumous *Let Noon Be Fair* (1966), modish excess. Formally, the debacle of "Leave Without Illusions" gave Motley the systematic training in the post-Steinbeck house style that has characterized so much popular American fiction, but which he had in his own experience fortuitously missed. Original Motley remains on page one of *Knock on Any Door,* in one of the passages he pleaded with his publishers not to excise. It echoes the eternal division in the history of the novel, between the news of what is happening and the vision of what really is going on, and stands by default as Motley's preface:

The sparrow sits on a telephone pole in the alley in the city.

The city is the world in microcosm.

The city lies in spendor and squalor. There are many doors to the city. Many things hide behind the many doors. More lives than one are lived in the city, more deaths than one are met within the city's gate.

The city doesn't change.

The people come and go, the visitors. They see the front yard.

But what of the city's back yard, and the alley? Who knows the lives and minds of the people who live in the alley?

Knock on any door down this street, in this alley.

CHAPTER SEVEN

John Updike since *Midpoint*

THE literary career of John Updike, beginning with his first book in 1958, spans nearly a quarter century of the most disruptive and transformative years in recent American history. The events which have taken place during Updike's tenure as one of the country's leading writers signal major changes in the American spirit: a confrontation with domestic disorder never before known in its history, the formation of an influential youth culture, a new sympathy to the plight of racial minorities, a strong emphasis on personal freedom over and above conventional morality and the traditions of responsibility, and the expression of violent resistance to a foreign war. That these factors had an effect upon the American imagination seems indisputable, since the artifacts which express that culture's aesthetic imagination—its fictions, poems, films, music, and art—all underwent radical transformations of theme and form during these times. In 1958, during the last sleepy year of the Eisenhower Administration, America had yet to read much of Kurt Vonnegut, Richard Brautigan, Donald Barthelme, or Ishmael Reed; it had not yet listened to the Beatles, the Beach Boys, Bob Dylan, or the other musicians who were to transform popular music as radically as Vonnegut changed the novel; pop art, conceptual art, and environmental art were movements yet unborn; Frank O'Hara's disarmingly conversational poems were yet to be widely printed.

In the years since 1958 Updike has published on the average one book every twelve months. His subject matter has always been contemporary American middle-class life; the life-styles of his characters are close to those of the country at large, and his fiction could hardly escape the radical changes in those lives. Moreover, Updike has been self-consciously and artistically retrospective: in 1971 he published an updated sequel to his second novel, titled *Rabbit Redux;* the year before that he surveyed the life of a fiction writer somewhat like himself in *Bech: A Book;* and in 1969 he had closed the decade with his booklength, introspective poem, *Midpoint,* where at age thirty-five he took inventory of the first half of his life. John Updike has matured and developed as a writer concurrently with the birth of a new American culture. His methods have been to grow with that culture, while maintaining a basic artistic conservativism which forms a helpful bridge from our present times to the recent, but aesthetically remote, past.

Updike's first novels, *The Poorhouse Fair*[1] and *Rabbit, Run,*[2] were such accurate portraits of fifties American culture that they quickly earned their author his reputation as the novelist of his times. Although projected a few decades into the future, *The Poorhouse Fair* voices the anguish a sensitive soul would rightly feel when faced with the blank materialism of the Eisenhower years. Updike shows us a microcosmic welfare state, where every temporal care of its retirement-age citizens is satisfied, except for the biggest one: their fear at confronting death. The state, Updike shows, has robbed the people of their faith, which he sees as the one comfort they might have when faced with death—as they are during every moment of existence in this old-age home. In this self-consciously microcosmic world, the administrator's shooting of a stray cat (which like the inmates clings tenaciously to life) occasions a judgment on the quality of life such a new society seeks:

Conner [the administrator of the home] had no regrets about ordering the animal killed. He wanted things *clean;* the world needed renewal, and this was a time of history when there were no cleansing wars or sweeping purges, when reform was slow, and decayed things were allowed to stand and rot themselves away. It was a vegetable world. Its theory was organic: perhaps old institutions in their dying could make fertile the chemical earth. So the gunshot ringing out, though a discord, pleased the rebel in Conner, the idealist, anxious to make space for the crystalline erections that in his heart he felt certain would arise, once his old people were gone. For the individual cat he felt nothing but sorrow. (p. 64)

Waiting only to die, Conner's charges have American health, but no heart, since the *mores* of their children's new society has taken that away from them. Though his first novel is heavily allegorical, Updike's indictment of that society is clear. His heavily stylized prose, noticed from the very first, takes root in the baroque quality of these old people's lives, and is played against the sterile efficiency of the world their prefects would impose.

Rabbit, Run is a more culturally immediate test of Updike's theme and style. His reaction against the new sterile society was now voiced by a child of that world, Harry "Rabbit" Angstrom, and Updike's stylistics became the vehicle for Rabbit's protest against a world which offered him no good. Harry, the former high school basketball star relegated to a life of selling kitchen gadgets in a dime store, feels that his own worth adds up to little more than the shabbiness of his wife, apartment, and broken ideals. There is little chance for success; and, as in the insipid television game shows, this life doesn't allow much room for tragedy. The stern faith of his childhood is replaced by the "ping-pong" religion of young Jack Eccles, the minister who feels happiest in the suburban drugstore, where

the poodle-cut girl behind the counter is in his Youth Group and two parishioners buying medicine or contraceptives or Kleenex hail him gaily. He feels at home in public places; he rests his wrists on the cold clean marble and orders a vanilla ice-cream soda with a scoop of maple-walnut ice cream, and drinks two Coca-Cola glasses full of delicious clear water before it comes. (p. 172)

In his critical collections *Assorted Prose*[3] and *Picked-Up Pieces*[4] Updike revealed one of his own personal interests to be religion; in characterizing Rabbit's dilemma in terms of the secularization of religion, Updike is making his own negative statement on the tenor of the times. His Rabbit would be a saint: aspiring to perfection in the little mundane things of life, Rabbit finds the world uncooperative. Unlike the artificially managed ideality of the high school basketball court, life is messy and unrewarding; the best he can do is to flee it. In the manner of Denis de Rougemont's *Love in the Western World* (a subject of Updike's commentary in *Assorted Prose*), Rabbit doubts his own existence, and can reaffirm it only in love. However, the very imperfections of the world which have caused his uneasiness refuse to give him an object worthy either of his eros or agape. In his review of de Rougemont's *Love Declared,* Updike analyzes what is Rabbit's ideal, the love-myth.

Her essence is *passion itself;* her concern is not with the possession, through love, of another person but with the prolongation of the lover's state of mind. Eros is allied with Thanatos rather than Agape; love becomes not a way of accepting and entering the world but a way of defying and escaping it. (p. 285)

But although Rabbit's quest fails, making him more antihero than hero, Updike insists that the shabby conditions of lower-middle-class American life are the true culprits.

The Centaur[5] and *Couples*[6] show Updike examining past and present, but expressing the same attitude toward life that he had developed in his earlier novels. The fear of death, as developed in *Rabbit, Run* and in the story "Pigeon Feathers" from the collection of that name,[7] is repeated in both novels. In each case, death is more than the cessation of physical life; it is the vacancy of beauty and value as well. In *The Centaur* Peter Caldwell is grateful for his father's (in the myth, Chiron's) gift of life. But the elder Caldwell's steps are marked by a mortality which only the parallel tales, modern and classic, can convey. The boy sees his father, the teacher, mocked, and the myths debased:

> "Zeus, Lord of the Sky; cloud-gathering king of the weather."
> "A lecherous muddler."
> "His bride Hera, patron of holy marriage."
> "The last time I saw her she was beating her servants because Zeus had not spent a night in her bed for a year. You know how Zeus first made love to her? As a cuckoo."
> "A hoopoe," Chiron corrected.
> "It was a silly cuckoo like in a clock. Tell me some more gods. I think they're so funny." (p. 25)

Although this novel was highly praised because of its coincidental rewriting of the Greek myth, the true mark of Updike's imagination is just the reverse: his parallel writing of a contemporary story, which tells a similar tale but from Updike's point of view. *Couples,* on the other hand, is explicitly quotidian. The subject of intermarital infidelity had great topical popularity in the 1960s, and the events of Updike's couples are here linked not to a classical myth, but instead to the day's news events. Yet ever present is the Puritan landscape Updike's moderns now occupy. His carpenter Piet Hanema alone recognizes the craftsmanship in their daily lives. He also has a vague feeling for their stern Calvinism, but not enough to keep him from the same fall into eros which damned Rabbit Angstrom. His lofty intentionality is lost amid the carnal, a theme Updike exploited throughout the first decade of his career. But again, his style argues against the harsh morality of his subject, celebrating instead the natural instincts of his characters, which too often run against their better fortunes. The simplest of physical acts occasions Updike's finest prose:

She pulled the elastic of his underpants toward her, eased it down and around. Her gaze became complacent. A cloud passingly blotted the sun. Sensing and fearing a witness, Piet looked upward and was awed as if by something inexplicable by the unperturbed onward motion of the fleet of blue-bellied clouds, ships with a single destination. The little eclipsing cloud burned gold in its tendrilous masts and stern. A cannon discharge of irridescence, and it passed.

Passed on safely above him. Sun was renewed in bold shafts on the cracked April earth, the sodden autumnal leaves, the new shoots coral in the birches and mustard on the larch boughs, the dropped needles drying, the tarpaper, their discarded clothes. (p. 54)

It is the hallmark of Updike's style in the 1960s that he can routinely insert one hundred words of stylistic exercise in finely wrought prose within the seconds that his lovers' clothing falls away. If his theme lacks purity and nobility, his style alone fulfills those roles, qualities which in a distant way anticipate the major literary disruptions of the coming years.

Midpoint was the occasion for Updike's reaffirming of what had already become his imaginative credo.[8] Deliberately self-reflective, in itself a trait of the innovative literature that appeared during the years of Updike's ascendency, the work subtly mocks itself and its own creation; the opening lines of *Midpoint* are spoken in the same voice as John Barth's "Autobiography: A Self-Recorded Fiction." The poem studies Updike's role at age thirty-five: half his life done and looking at the present for what he has found it to be. The world is still a troublesome place, even in terms of scientific specifics. In Section III, "The Dance of the Solids," the poet argues that "Solidity emerges as intricate and giddy," an analog to the moral dilemma of his characters in fiction: "Textbooks and Heaven only are Ideal;/Solidity is an imperfect state" (pp. 18, 20). As in *The Centaur,* he cannot see his life as perfectly organized as that of his elders:

> Father, as old as you when I was four,
> I feel the restlessness of nearing death
> But lack your manic passion to endure,
> Your Stoic fortitude and Christian faith.
> Remember, at the blackboard, factoring?
> My life at midpoint seems a string of terms
> In which an error clamps the hidden spring
> Of resolution cancelling confirms. (pp. 35–36)

What troubles the poet is a higher sensitivity to the erosion of life's values. "An easy Humanism plagues the land," begins Section V, the conclusion. "I choose to take an otherworldly stand." His mentors in this stand are again theological:

> Praise *Kierkegaard,* who splintered Hegel's creed
> Upon the rock of existential need;
> Praise *Barth,* who told how saving Faith can flow
> From Terror's oscillating Yes and No. (p. 38)

Rabbit Angstrom lived in a world which refused him grounds for the leap of faith, which sentenced him to the mere erotic; hence today Updike finds that "Apocalypse is in; mad Eros drives/The continents upon a shoal of lives" (p. 39). Yet Updike has forever admitted that a resolution to this problem would destroy the very tension which he sees as human life itself. Mortality cannot be fused with the eternal, the ideal; from his favorite theologian, Karl Barth, Updike argues that "The god who stood at the end of some human way . . . would not be God." What Updike clearly prefers, from the portraits of ministers and sinners he has drawn in several books, is Barth's diety. "The real God," Updike insists, "the God men do not invent, is *totaliter aliter*—Wholly Other. We cannot reach him; only He can reach us" (*Assorted Prose,* pp. 273-74). But this very strategy outmaneuvers the "death of God" theology so prevalent in the 1960s; if man does not invent God, he clearly cannot kill him. The religious center of Updike's imagination remains conservative, running counter to the trend of the times. But once properly freed of the influence of the ideal, finitude becomes a matter for celebration, a concluding note of hope for *Midpoint:*

> The meanwhile, let us live as islanders
> Who pluck what fruit the lowered branch proffers.
> Each passing moment makes a tender face;
> Nothing has to be, but is by Grace.
> Attend to every sunset; greet the dawn
> That combs with spears of shade the glistening lawn.
> Enjoy the slanting morning, upright noon,
> Declining day, and swollen leprous moon. (p. 40)

Updike's role as a fictive stylist has been to celebrate such sunsets and dawns; in *Bech: A Book* he takes an extended look at that role,[9] giving the principles of *Midpoint* an experiential test according to his own professional life. Henry Bech is not a transcription of Updike; rather he is described as an amalgamation of many serious writers of the time: Norman Mailer, Saul Bellow, Philip Roth, Bernard Malamud, and J. D. Salinger. The part of Bech derivative of Updike is described as "something Waspish, theological, scared, and insulatingly ironical" (p. v). Running throughout the seven collected stories which form this novel is the reminder that Bech is in a writer's block, and indeed may have dried up. The point at issue is his inability to finish a third novel. Although the self-scrutiny is reminiscent of *Midpoint,* the logistics of Bech's career hardly conform to Updike's. What does conform is more important: Bech believes his own spring has run dry because of the spiritually exhausting nature of this theme, that "Actuality is a running impoverishment of possibility'' (p. 69). But more striking are Bech's misgivings about his literary style, which like his theme runs directly parallel to Updike's writing. At this turn the author himself breaks away, exclaiming, "Enough. Like Bech, we reach a point where words seem horrible, maggots on the carcass of reality, feeding, proliferating; we seek peace in silence and reduction" (p. 130). Bech's style and theme have taken him to the ultimacies of both: silence and death. "The essence of the matter, he saw, is dread. Death hung behind everything, a real skeleton about to leap through a door in these false walls of books" (p. 110). The lesson of *Bech: A Book* is that one of Updike's imaginative values, the Kierkegaardian "dread," is shown as having reached its limits of efficacy for contemporary American culture. Henry Bech, as a writer, has faced that culture more directly than Updike's previous heroes; likewise, he is a master himself of the style which has been Updike's last resort. As Updike begins the 1970s, *Bech* is his admission that large parts of his own aesthetic may have been exhausted by time and circumstance.

Bech: A Book and *Rabbit Redux*[10] are not among Updike's strongest works, but they are valuable because they show their author's recognition that certain styles and thematics of the 1960s had been exhausted, much as John Barth's essay, "The Literature of Exhaustion," had argued a few years before. Henry Bech, we recall, shared traits of many mainstream fiction writers, among them Updike, Bellow, and Malamud. Surrounding the publication of *Bech* were curiously retrospective novels by all three authors: Updike's *Rabbit Redux,* Bellow's *Mr. Sammler's Planet,* and Malamud's *The Tenants.* All three books are strikingly similar in both theme and technique. They rely heavily on content (in a day when newer writers such as Ronald Sukenick, Donald Barthelme, and Steve Katz were disclaiming any interest in content at all), and within their own aesthetic order argue for a more orderly world (when Thomas Pynchon was displaying the chaotic artificiality of all order). These were just the standards which critics of the time were ascribing to "the death of the novel" and "the literature of exhaustion." For Susan Sontag, Norman Mailer, Leslie Fiedler, Norman Podhoretz, and many other traditionalist critics, the end of the 1960s looked like the end of the novel. "The discoveries of modern physics and of behavioral psychology have all but destroyed the old certainty of the human ordering of experience," wrote Louis Rubin; therefore "there can be no solid basis, whether in finite matter or in human reason, upon which the novelist can erect his commentary." Content, or meaning, was just the part of the traditional novel which needed such a stable world.

Looking at his protagonist, Rabbit Angstrom, ten years later,

Updike admits that the culture has eclipsed him. There has been a dissipation of energy; whereas a decade before Rabbit could at least be antiheroic, in 1969 he is simply pathetic:

Thirty-six years old and he knows less than when he started. With the difference that now he knows how little he'll always know. He'll never know how to talk Chinese or how screwing an African princess feels. The six o'clock news is all about peace, all about emptiness: some bald man plays with little toys to show the docking and undocking maneuvers, and then a panel talks about the significance of this for the next five hundred years. They keep mentioning Columbus but as far as Rabbit can see it's the exact opposite: Columbus flew blind and hit something, these guys see exactly where they're aiming and it's a big round nothing. (p. 22)

The materialism of 1950s middle-class life was at least concrete and definable; Rabbit had his own grace as an athlete and aesthete to posit against it. But the 1970s strike him as inexplicable: he can't possibly understand the physics of space, nor can he invent a mythology for it. Like Saul Bellow's Artur Sammler, the moralist, and like Bernard Malamud's Harry Lesser, the literary craftsman, Rabbit feels outdated; "He put his life into rules he feels melting away now" (p. 53). Like both Sammler and Lesser he is confronted by symbols of the new cultural times, a black activist and a young, militant white girl. He tries to explain how he is a veteran himself of such aesthetic wars. "No kidding," he argues, "I once took that inner light trip and all I did was bruise my surroundings. Revolution, or whatever, is just a way of saying a mess is fun. Well, it *is* fun, for a while, as long as somebody else has laid in supplies. A mess is luxury, is all I mean" (p. 172). But Rabbit has misjudged the energy of the time, mistaking his own former vague dissatisfaction for the current active upheavals. Moreover, he has been unsexed by the failure of his own revolt. Now he complains against "Always these demands and impossible expectations" of the newly militant female sexuality. He would rather retire from life. A linotypist, the new computer typesetting puts him out of work, and he winds up as unproductive as Harry Lesser, and as obsolete as Mr. Sammler.

Rabbit Redux shows two things: that Updike's classic protagonist has been outdated by the new thematics of the time, and that the story of his present life does not provide the makings of good Updike-style fiction. It is best regarded as Updike's experiment with his old themes and techniques amid the new times; the result of the experiment is that they do not mix. Therefore it is no surprise that Updike's next books take a decided turn in thematics, in order to maintain both the author's stylistics and his commitment to the quotidian facts and experiences of current American life. The biggest development in Updike's writing displayed in his collection *Museums and Women and Other Stories* is a self-conscious reflectiveness about style.[11] "Set together, the two words are seen to be mutually transparent; the E's, the M's blend—the M's framing and squaring the structure lend resonance and a curious formal weight to the M central in the creature, which it dominates like a dark core winged with flitting syllables. Both words hum. Both suggest radiance, antiquity, mystery, and duty." By considering first the *words* of his title story, and by following from there to the theme which emerges from them, Updike adopts the new decade's most emphatic belief for fiction: that the ultimate reality lies not in the described action of the story, but rather in the shape and sounds of the words. Moreover Updike is self-conscious about his role as writer of the fiction; by attending to such details as technique, he remains ever present with the words, instead of disappearing behind the screen of narrative. Such a transition makes the most of Updike's highly stylized writing; instead of being a distracting and sometimes disharmonious burden, as his early critics complained, style here becomes the very point of his fiction.

Museums and Women is Updike's broadest collection, reprinting stories passed over by earlier volumes and dating back to 1960. The first of these, "The Sea's Green Sameness," begins a section (safely kenneled in the rear) titled "Other Modes": experiments in prose which were in tune with or even ahead of their times, but which their author did not admit to the canon of his collected works until this late date. "I write on this beach. Let us say, then, that I am a writer on the beach. It was once considered bad manners to admit anything of the sort, just as people walking to and from the bathroom were supposed to be invisible," the author observes at the beginning; "but this is a rude age" (p. 159). Rude for manners, but not for writing techniques, since Updike's self- consciousness enables him to make style his theme, which in one act solves the problems of exhaustion forecast in *Bech* and evidenced in *Rabbit Redux*. Updike's ploy is the same used by John Barth, Ronald Sukenick, and the others who felt this same inadequacy with the old conventions. Updike's achievement, however, is that he already was a master stylist, waiting only for this new period of license to exercise his true gifts.

Updike's new self-consciousness allows him to use his stylistics in a newly responsible way. In one story, "The Day of the Dying Rabbit," he casts his protagonist as a creative photographer, whose own imagination visualizes things in the terms of Updike's language, as he takes photographs of "grass and sand and shadows, close-up, using the ultraviolet filter, trying to get what may be ungettable, the way the shadow edges stagger from grain to grain on the sand, and the way some bent-over grass blades draw circles around themselves, to keep time away" (pp. 32–33). Here the thematics of theology are replaced by a simple aesthetic problem, voiced by an aesthetitian in terms proper to his (and to Updike's) art. But Updike also reveals a movement away from religion as the necessary counterpart of his natural descriptions; early in his title story he makes a distinction, quite new for the imaginative center of his writing, that "What we seek in museums is the opposite of what we seek in churches—the consoling sense of previous visitation. In museums, rather, we seek the untouched, the never-before-discovered; and it is their final unsearchability that leads us to hope, and return" (p. 12).

Both *Museums and Women* and *A Month of Sundays*[12] are in this sense museum works. The secularization of our culture now interests Updike more than its religious elements; and in terms of structure, he has discarded strong narrative in favor of a quiet, hopeful examination of subjects in stasis—almost as if they are tucked away for study in a museum. Most of the stories in *Museums and Women* are static affairs: the examination of an "orphaned" swimming pool, of a curious street corner, or of a carol sing at church. Ministers per se interest Updike less than the mundane business of what to do with a disgraced minister (disgraced for secular reasons), or simply the day-to-day running of the church. His collection gives us portraits of people who are like still-life subjects: nothing happens to them in the story, other than the author finding them as themselves. When action does take place in these stories, it is lethargic at worst and retrospective at best; Updike's old characters, the couples of Tarbox, the commuters to Boston, are tired and sad. Updike's real interest is in the landscape. He devotes an entire story, "Plumbing," to the history of his vacated house, which dates back over two hundred years and will probably last several hundred more. "All around us," he concludes, "we are outlasted" (p. 155).

In his earlier work, Updike drew thematic attention to sexuality. But as the treatment of that topic in American culture has become more open and bold, Updike's handling of it has changed. The candor with which he handled sexuality in *Rabbit, Run,* including explicit scenes of masturbation and fellatio, earned Updike the early reputation as an uninhibited, even salacious writer. But as we have seen, in this writer's early work sexuality is inevitably linked to religion. Rabbit's sexual yearnings are meant to be the first step in the Kierkegaardian progression to faith. But in Updike's most recent books sexuality stands alone as an explicitly secular event, much as it has come to in current American culture, which has learned to treat it as a physically exuberant act and little more. The first indication of this change in Updike's attitude comes with the closing section of *Museums and Women,* which includes several stories about a married couple, the Maples, who have been featured in Updike's work dating back to their first appearance in *The New Yorker* in 1956. What has distinguished this couple has been their love; through all types of situational distractions and even catastrophes, Updike has shown them as steadfast in their union. With *Museums and Women,* however, we see the times drawing them apart. Beginning with "Marching Through Boston," where Joan Maple finds an affinity for the civil rights movement which her husband Dick cannot share, we see them drawn apart, until the erotic separates them forever—Dick abstaining from sex altogether after an initial affair, while Joan remains with a string of lovers. The sexuality is purely a cultural phenomenon. In 1979 Updike collected all the Maples stories for a paperback; not surprisingly, the last piece finds them divorced.[13]

When sexuality was not so explicit in the culture, Updike treated it in terms of religion; but for the 1970s, the author takes it on its own. *Marry Me,* his novel of 1976, extends the same theme and technique.[14] Sexuality represents simply itself. Jerry Conant and Sally Mathias are physical and not metaphysical lovers. They desert their families for shallow reasons, and their inconclusiveness is shown by the book's three different endings.

A Month of Sundays is the ultimate statement of the secularization (and self-conscious stylization) of John Updike's fiction. Of his many books and stories that contain ministers, it is the only book so far with a churchman as the central character. And of all Updike's novels, except perhaps for *Bech: A Book,* it contains the least purely religious impulse. One reason is that the story concerns Rev. Thomas Marshfield's history of estrangement from the church, in favor of a string of adulterous affairs with his church organist and several women parishioners. A sign of definite theological change in Updike's imagination is seen in his move from the uncompromising Karl Barth to the more liberal Paul Tillich; the latter's epigraph, "This principle of soul, universally and individually, is the principle of ambiguity," stands at the head of *A Month of Sundays* and informs its every chapter. Tillich, as Updike would surely know, was a follower of Frederich Schleiermacher, whose theology made a pact with secularity: for each theological hypothesis, Schleiermacher would be sure to follow with a totally phenomenological argument, as if the spiritual could not exist without its counterpart in the physical world. Karl Barth rejected this method, insisting that any contact with the temporal world would corrupt the transcendence of his ultimate argument. The tendency in Updike's earlier fiction, although following the method of double proof, still favored the spiritual over the physical, often with a

Barthian toughness—particularly in *Rabbit, Run* with the contrasting ministers Kruppenbach and Eccles.

Rev. Tom Marshfield has neither the stern religion of Kruppenbach or the socially religious eagerness of Eccles. Instead, he has followed the ambiguity of the soul to its grounding in the physical. At the same time Updike has made the novel in which Marshfield lives a highly self-reflective affair. Taken to a retreat house for a month's recuperation after the scandals of his pastorhood, Marshfield is given the task of writing each day; the results are the thirty-one chapters of this book. Within these pages he tells the story of his ostensible decline and fall, but in an eminently self-conscious manner: "This is fun! First you whittle the puppets, then you move them around" (p. 12). Certain sentences are painful for him to write and to read; others excite him sexually to the point of masturbation. The text becomes as vital as his own sensations; Updike has found the way of animating his own act of writing shared by his more innovative contemporaries—Sukenick, Federman, and Katz. We are constantly reminded of the text before us, and of the living writer's hand in it, down to a musing about errors in the typescript—which are not distractions, for Updike is showing how some of the reality of his story is in the text itself.

Marshfield must create his own religion from the secular history of his life, for the Bible has been banned from this psychological retreat. Working with these materials, Marshfield creates only the second half of a Schleiermacher/Tillich argument, justifying the record of his own conduct in the world:

> Let us turn from Holy Writ to the world that surrounds us. Wherein does the modern American man recover his sense of worth, not as dogged breadwinner and economic integer, but as romantic minister and phallic knight, as personage, embodiment, and hero? In adultery. (p. 46)

Like a fictive artist, Marshfield sees that he has been creating his own life as a fiction, moving characters about to suit his whim, as with the family of his illicit lover:

> Gerry, Frankie, Julie, Barry—how small remoteness has whittled them. They seem dolls I can play with, putting them now in this, now in that obscene position. I put the Frankie doll in a nightie, and lie her in bed, and spread her jointed legs, and set the Gerry doll on top, while the Julie and Barry dolls sleep the dreamless sleep of the safe and inorganic. I look down upon the copulating dolls by removing a section of the roof no bigger than a chessboard. The Frankie doll's painted eyes stare up at me blindly. I am too big to see. (p. 178)

He has been sent to this retreat house, then, to take him out of the world he has been manipulating and creating. His sole contact with the moveable world is Mrs. Prynne, administratrix of the institution and sole reader of his pages. "As my end approaches," Marshfield writes her, "everything grows vaporous, my future and my past are the same green cloud, and only you are solid, only you have substance; I fall toward you as a meteorite toward the earth, as a comet toward the sun" (p. 217).

The minister's triumph, and the ultimate turn of Updike's imagination, is to make Marshfield's prose victorious over Mrs. Prynne. The novel ends with her seduction according to the same terms as his earlier achievements, only now accomplished by his self-created words. Whether as a meteor to earth (Tillich) or as a comet toward the sun (Barth), Updike has placed his value in the ability of the writer to successfully create his own world. His minister now is not a reflector of the heavenly realm (as an older fictionist might describe another reality), but as the fashioner of his own reality, the central point won by the innovations in fiction during Updike's tenure as a major American writer.

CHAPTER EIGHT

The Dramatization of Kurt Vonnegut

LIKE so many novelists before him, Kurt Vonnegut chose middle life as the time to go into drama. Whether or not his feelings ultimately prove true, it is a matter of record that Vonnegut regarded the publication of *Slaughterhouse-Five* (1969) as a culmination of his first twenty years in fiction. After five novels of trying, he could admit "I've finished my war book now. The next one I write is going to be fun."[1] At the University of Michigan he was more explicit: "The thing I just wrote," he told his audience, "is my masterpiece. The rest of it is going to be crap from now on."[2] As it happened, the projected novel, *Breakfast of Champions,* was at least temporarily abandoned because his mind was elsewhere, more specifically in the theater.[3] *Happy Birthday, Wanda June* (1970–71), as he explains in its preface, "is what I did when I was forty-seven years old," when his professional and personal lives were taking a new direction.[4] The play "follows *Slaughterhouse-Five* chronologically and emotionally," he told a reporter in the morning after its opening.[5] Therefore even as Vonnegut returns to fiction, as did Twain, James, Howells, Fitzgerald, Hemingway, and so many others, the event of *Happy Birthday, Wanda June* marks a change in his vision, in content as well as form.

There are logical reasons in Vonnegut's career why he should look to the stage. In 1969, before *Wanda June* was under way, Vonnegut speculated that he would like to "try a play," because "There's not much set-building [as for a novelist] and not much work with characteristics that you would have with a short story or novel. Other people are doing that work."[6] For a writer described as a Wellsian novelist of ideas, drama would indeed be inviting, where actors, directors, and designers do so much to flesh out the material.[7] But there were personal reasons as well:

Reprinted in part from *Players* 50, copyright 1975, pp. 62–64.

in nearly every interview he gave at the time Vonnegut emphasized the communal nature of theater, calling the company not just his associates but his "new family." According to his preface, the play was done near the end of middle life, "when my six children were children no more. It was a time of change, of good-bye and good-bye and good-bye. My big house was becoming a museum of vanished childhoods—of my vanished young manhood as well" (p. [vii]). Excisions from his corrected transcript[8] show that this was a time of even greater personal turmoil; in a comment which remains in the text, Vonnegut speaks reflectively, claiming:

> I was supposedly a right-handed person, but I found myself using my left hand more and more. It became the hand that did most of the giving and taking for me. I asked my older brother what he knew of this. He said that I had been an ambidextrous infant. I had been taught to favor my right hand.
> "I'm left-handed now, and I'm through with novels," I told him. "I'm writing a play. It's plays from now on." (p. [vii])

The idea to be dramatized, the same idea at the center of Vonnegut's personal life following the "expiation" of *Slaughterhouse-Five,* is that of pacifism. "What do you say about a massacre?" Vonnegut asked in that work, as he had been implicitly asking in all his fiction since 1950. Trying to answer that question, Vonnegut had transformed social ethics (*Player Piano* and *God Bless You, Mr. Rosewater*), philosophies of man and God (*Mother Night* and *Cat's Cradle*), and even space and time (*The Sirens of Titan* and *Slaughterhouse-Five*). But in his novels there was no material solution, since "there is nothing intelligent to say about a massacre"; all is "short and jumbled and jangled," making sense only when we share Billy Pilgrim's imaginative transformation of death, which is no less than Vonnegut's supratemporal reinvention of his world, where time is relative and historical catastrophes can be sidestepped at will.[9]

Happy Birthday, Wanda June begins with the same problem. Introducing Colonel Looseleaf Harper, the man who dropped the A-bomb on Nagasaki, "killing seventy-four thousand people in a flash," Vonnegut shows him as vastly inarticulate on the subject of killing. "I dunno, boy," he shrugs, finally just muttering, "It was a bitch" (pp. 2-3). An articulate killer is on hand, however: Harold Ryan, a Hemingway manqué who has killed "perhaps two hundred men in various wars of sorts—as a professional soldier," and "thousands of other animals as well—for sport" (p. 2). Like Odysseus and his crew, Ryan has been lost for eight years, and returns with Harper to find his home filled with suitors and his wife about to marry a doctor: a healer, and moreover, a pacifist. But unlike other Vonnegut heroes, Ryan and Harper must neither transform nor reinvent the world. To their great dismay the world has been transformed already. Harper senses the difference, although he can hardly express it. "You know what gets me?" he asks Ryan, "How all the magazines show tits today" (p. 44). He is also surprised at the obscenity accepted in speech, and decides "Something very big must have happened while we were out of the country" (p. 46). He gropes for an answer, suspecting that "Something very important about sex must have happened while were gone" (p. 50). But the moon landings also impress him, and it takes the more articulate Ryan to draw a conclusion: "The moon. The new heroism—put a village idiot into a pressure cooker, seal it up tight, and shoot him at the moon" (p. 52). The times have proven Ryan's machismo heroism out of date; a transformation in sexual mores has occurred, as an index to even greater changes, and Ryan must now face the test of his own ethic by a society which has left him behind.

Like the returning hero Odysseus, Ryan encounters changes in his own home. There is a weak, ineffectual suitor, the vacuum cleaner salesman Herb Shuttle, but also the intellectually formidable Dr. Norbert Woodly. His wife Penelope has changed, earning a master's degree in English literature, to which Ryan remarks, "What a pity! Educating a beautiful woman is like pouring honey into a fine Swiss watch. Everything stops" (p. 69). When he tells her this to her face, adding that "The body of a woman should feel like a hot water bottle filled with Devonshire cream" (p. 113), Penelope objects, "You leave me so—so without—without *dignity*" (p. 123). She has changed since the time he picked her up in a drive-in restaurant, almost a side order to his raw hamburger and onion eaten like apple. "When I was a carhop," she admits, "I didn't feel much more than a fish would. But I've been sensitized. I have ideas now—and solid information. I know a lot more now—and a lot of it has to do with *you*." Her sensitivity is in truth a new sensibility, the recognition that the "whole concept of heroism" has changed (p. 130). While Penelope articulates it, Colonel Looseleaf Harper is slowly discovering the new sensibility himself. After his friend Ryan has smashed Woodly's two-hundred-year-old violin, he puts his feelings into words:

. . . after you busted that thing, I got to thinking, "Jesus—maybe I'll start the violin again." That was a mean, childish thing—busting that violin. That didn't belong to Woodly. That belonged to *everybody*. Maybe he would have sold it to me, and I could have had some fun. Then I could sell it to somebody else, and he could have some fun. (p. 160)

To this radically new principle, the conservation of joy, Harper adds that he missed his own chance for true heroism at Nagasaki: "If I *hadn't* done it. If I'd said to myself, 'Screw it. 'I'm going to let all those people down there live' " (p. 161). He explains to Ryan, "You could have been the manufacturer of that violin there, even though you don't know how to make a violin, just by not busting it up. I would have been the father of all those people in Nagasaki, and the mother, too, just by not dropping the bomb" (p. 162). Penelope completes the transformation: "the new heroes," she tells her husband, are those "who refuse to fight" (p. 176).

Ryan cannot understand. The world seems turned on its head, his seemingly logical values paradoxically reversed. Vonnegut faces the same challenge in demonstrating to the audience how not fighting is heroic, how not killing is creative. His solution is peculiarly dramatic, extending part of the action to Heaven, where various characters (including one killed by Ryan) discuss the ideality which supposedly justifies our conduct on earth. Here Wanda June herself, "A lisping eight-year-old . . . as cute as Shirley Temple" is guide:

Hello, I am Wanda June. Today was going to be my birthday, but I was hit by an ice-cream truck before I could have my party. I am dead now. I am in Heaven. That is why my parents did not pick up the cake at the bakery. I am not mad at the ice-cream truck driver, even though he was drunk when he hit me. It didn't hurt much. It wasn't even as bad as the sting of a bumblebee. I am really *happy* here. It's so much fun. I am glad the driver was drunk. If he hadn't been, I might not have got to Heaven for years and years and years. I would have had to go to high school first, and then beauty college. I would have had to get married and have babies and everything. Now I can just play and play and play. Any time I want any pink cotton candy I can have some. Everybody up here is happy—the animals and the dead soldiers and people who went to the electric chair and everything. They're all glad for whatever sent them here. Nobody is mad. We're all too busy playing shuffleboard. So if you think of killing somebody, don't worry about it. Just go ahead and do it. Whoever you do it to should kiss you for doing it. The soldiers up here just love the shrapnel and the tanks and the bayonets and the dum dums that let them play shuffleboard all the time—and drink beer. (pp. 53–55)

Her playmate is Maj. Siegfried von Konigswald, "The Beast of Yugoslavia," who as a Nazi SS officer killed more men than even Harold Ryan, before being strangled to death by Ryan himself. But in Heaven all is forgiven, where everyone simply plays shuffleboard: Hitler, Albert Einstein, Mozart, Jack the Ripper, Walt Disney, and even Jesus Christ. "It was almost worth the trip," says von Konigswald, "to find out that Jesus Christ in Heaven was just another guy playing shuffleboard. I like his sense of humor, though—you know? He's got a blue-and-gold warm-up jacket he wears. You know what it says on the back? 'Pontius Pilate Athletic Club' '' (p. 136).

Vonnegut's view of Heaven is amusing until we discover it is not his view at all, but that of his character Harold Ryan, who uses it as a justification for killing. He shrugs off the death of Harper's mother-in-law by claiming ''She's up in Heaven now. She didn't hear. She is experiencing nothing but pure happiness. There's nothing nicer than that'' (p. 121). Looseleaf Harper had adopted the same easy ethic at Nagasaki—''I sent 'em to Heaven instead''—but now, he confesses, ''I don't think there *is* one'' (p. 162). Penelope argues the point with Ryan, that his notion of honor is ''all balled up in your head with death. When you talk of these animals, one by one, you don't just talk of killing them. You honored them with death. Harold—it is not honor to be killed.'' Her argument is that ''It's still just death, the absence of life—no honor at all'' (p. 174). Ryan's Heaven is something else. If the audience doubts Vonnegut's intention, it need only glance at the dramatist's one concession to the printed page, the play's program. There the title device, repeated in book form on the dust jacket, features the lettering of Wanda June's birthday cake thrust out of line not by a shuffleboard stick, but by a devil's pitchfork. It has been Ryan all along who has inverted values, and Vonnegut the dramatist who finally straightens them out.

To complete his critique of Ryan and all he stands for, Vonnegut offers some internal argument. Mildred Ryan, Harold's former wife, reveals that his machismo sexuality was mostly bluff; and his most immediate admirer, Herb Shuttle, is depicted as having homosexual tendencies. But the play's larger dramatic form and thematic structure are the true measures of Vonnegut's success. A self-admitted problem in his fiction, the inability to articulate the sense of a massacre, is evident in the character of Looseleaf Harper, whose fumbling manner of speech is seized upon as a major feature of the play, becoming a positive rather than negative feature. Harold Ryan, as central character, fumbles too; and his clumsiness is just as integral to the plot—in his ethical obsolescence he cannot even shoot straight enough to kill himself.

Vonnegut's most important development, however, lies not with his characters, but with the world they inhabit. In his previous fictions, that world was the villain, limiting man by such larger forces as technology, propensity for evil, or the simple realities of space and time. *Happy Birthday, Wanda June* is innovative in content as well as form, because it is the first time Vonnegut makes the world essentially right. Other Vonnegut heroes—Paul Proteus, Malachi Constant, Howard Campbell, John (of *Cat's Cradle*), Eliot Rosewater, and Billy Pilgrim—had left society behind, creating their own imaginative worlds. In Vonnegut's play, however, an already transformed society leaves Harold Ryan behind. The American 1960s, Kurt Vonnegut shows, have had their effect—both on his art and on life itself.

The shift in Vonnegut's art seems tied strongly to the drama, for in a passage excised from the play's preface he described the plot of what he was considering his "next" novel, *Breakfast of Champions.* Earlier interviews confirm the story of a Pontiac dealer who discovers one day that everybody else is a robot, and that he is the only creature in the universe with free will, placed on earth by God as a novel experiment. The book's epigraph, Vonnegut here reveals, would be taken from *Job:* "When He hath tried me, I shall come forth as gold."[10] Once again an innovative hero would strive against a static world, as do the protagonists of Vonnegut's first five novels[11]; but for the preface to *Wanda June,* comments on *Breakfast* in its original state were removed. Vonnegut's play, then, is most emphatically written with a different vision, of an environment changing faster than its traditionalist hero.

Perhaps the world in stasis was a necessary part of Vonnegut's earlier fiction: but *Happy Birthday, Wanda June* stands as an interesting example of how dramatic form can develop and transform a writer's vision. Elements of this revised vision are evident in *Slapstick; or, Lonesome No More,*[12] Vonnegut's first novel since *Breakfast of Champions,* which was in turn the first book he'd written under the pressure of his massive and sometimes mystifying fame. An integral part of *Breakfast* was Vonnegut's mental housecleaning, the sweeping out of twenty years' worth of themes and techniques, characters and ideas. His imaginary family for all those years—Eliot Rosewater, Kilgore Trout, the citizens of Ilium, New York, and Midland City, Indiana—were set free by their creator, who described himself as Count Tolstoi freeing his serfs in favor of a newer life for both.

But Vonnegut's artificial family was never more than just a portion of his art. His novels always included healthy doses of the familiar, mundane world. Vonnegut gathered details and events from his own life as well, such as his Indiana childhood, his wartime experiences, and his work as a publicist for General Electric, until they formed a mythology through all his books. Long before *Slaughterhouse-Five* made him famous, it was clear that Kurt Vonnegut was making a work of art out of his own life. While others said the novel might be dying, Vonnegut lived the life of fiction, keeping both himself and his novels alive and intact. But in the years since his first great public success (1969–1970), his life of fiction has been a profitably self-dramatized affair.

"This is the closest I will ever come to writing an autobiography," he begins in *Slapstick,* which was published explicitly without the familiar "Jr." of his name. Without any of his old characters and with none of his familiar themes, Vonnegut's novel nevertheless returns to the greatest strength of this writer's art: the ability to project the big and little concerns of his own life into the field of imaginary action. What might otherwise seem depressingly meaningless becomes what Vonnegut calls "grotesque, situational poetry"—the slapstick ballet that artists such as Laurel and Hardy (to whom this book is dedicated) made of an otherwise vexing life.

Writing a book in 1976, Vonnegut finds much in life to lament. His own family, so long in the center of his self-proclaimed middle-class existence, has been scattered across the planet—a planet which, moreover, Vonnegut fears is dying. His closest sibling and only sister, described here as the ideal reader of his books, died in the 1950s; her absence haunts this novel. His "home," Indianapolis, bears few traces of the once prosperous Vonnegut family. A trip back there with his brother Bernard, for the funeral of their last close Indiana relative, becomes the frame for *Slapstick,* a dream about the best and worst possibilities in life.

Families are at the heart of all these possibilities. In this prologue Vonnegut discusses the inadequacy of love and marriage as sole satisfiers of human needs, and how instead he's found better comfort in "common decency" and the warmth of large, close families. Both, however, are disappearing from our planet, with the result that two-person relationships are forced to do the work of grandparents, aunts, uncles, nephews, nieces, and cousins scattered so far away. So he uses the freedom of fiction to dream up a better reality, a set of new conventions more appropriate to present needs.

Vonnegut's working title for this novel was "The Relatives," which is what his theme is about. His main character, Wilbur Swain, is the last president of the United States, whose political program nearly saved the nation. He assigns random collective middle names to all citizens so that problems from social welfare to personal loneliness could be solved by artificially extended families, who would care for their own and provide for the common good. Swain's plan follows the natural inclination of people to band together in folk societies, following common interests as simple as the Mercedes-Benz Club of North America and as complex as the American Bar Association. The novel plots the rise and eventual dominance of these families, from their implementation as an artificial scheme to their evolution into anthropologically valid units as the nation itself collapses. "The Raspberries," we learn about one of the arbitrarily named families, "are food-gatherers, mainly living in and around the ruins of the New York Stock Exchange. They fish off docks. They mine for canned goods. They pick fruits and berries they find. They grow their own tomatoes and potatoes, and radishes, and little more.'' What first unites these groups is unimportant, as arbitrary as the cars they drive or professions they serve; what's important, Vonnegut argues, is that people need an excuse—apart from the usual one of common defense and aggression—for coming together and working toward the common purpose of comfortable survival in an often ridiculous universe.

Slapstick is a deceptively short and simple book. Its readability should not distract one from the fact that Vonnegut has found a fictional situation which considers serious human problems, just as the dramatic context of *Happy Birthday, Wanda June* provided a more timely structure for his statements on the American 1960s. Life, Vonnegut knows, keeps testing us far beyond our limits of control, and he long ago abandoned the doctrine of free will lest it tax us beyond all humanly bearable responsibility. It often seems the universe *is* booby-trapped against us. But the lesson of such slapstick comedians as Laurel and Hardy, Vonnegut argues, is that against all the tests of their "limited agility and intelligence . . . they did their best with every test. They never failed to bargain in good faith with their destinies," however ridiculous, "and were screamingly adorable and funny on that account." Against the insipid madness of life, that's how the Vonnegut who moves beyond *Slaughterhouse-Five* chooses to be: unalienated, self-effacing, funny, and comforting.

CHAPTER NINE

Donald Barthelme's Art of Collage

IN 1970, as his popular and academic reputation was growing, Donald Barthelme was given feature treatment by the Sunday *New York Times Magazine*. Richard Schickel's "Freaked Out on Barthelme" combined an interview with description and criticism to form an essay which both clarified and obscured Barthelme's art, anticipating the praises of Charles Thomas Samuels, William H. Gass, and others, but also forecasting the objections raised by Alfred Kazin, Pearl K. Bell, Nathan Scott, and the others who have disparaged Barthelme's short fiction.

The key to Schickel's thesis was Barthelme's comment, "The principle of collage is the central principle of all art in the twentieth century in all media." Schickel concluded that "if you come away from one of his works confused, terribly aware of it as a jumble of images and ideas, you will have caught his basic drift."[1] Citing the story "Brain Damage" as an example, Schickel argued that "It is a collage of the kind of stuff we might find if we peeked into any modern mind: a man finds an important book in a funny place, a famous waiter dies, Barthelme's past as a newspaperman is evoked, there is an odd anthropological report on an imaginary civilization, other bits and pieces of *dreck*."[2] From Barthelme's materials Schickel drew a conventional, moralistic meaning: "I think he thinks collage is the central artistic mode of our time because a brain-damaged society cannot 'get things together' any more tightly, rationally than the collage implies."[3] It is a short step to Alfred Kazin's condemnation of Barthelme's art as a mode of writing which "operates by counter-measures only, and the system that is his own joy to attack permits him what an authoritarian system always permits its lonely dissenters: the sense of their own weakness." Kazin concludes that "Barthelme sentences us to the complicity with the system that he suffers from more than anyone."[4] More praiseworthy is the older-style

Nabokov, who has at least "saved *us* from being always at the mercy of the age."[5]

Both Schickel the publicist and Kazin the critic mistake the point of Barthelme's art: that his collages of words, ideas, and graphic representations are not intellectual comments or moral judgments, but rather are *made objects*. As William Carlos Williams emphasized for this style of writing, "It isn't what [the author] *says* that counts as a work of art, it's what he makes."[6] As an aesthetic principle, it's as applicable to Barthelme's work as to the theory of collage itself. The collagist draws together objects from many different contexts, and places them together to make a new object—not necessarily to comment on the sources of his many pieces, of which he well may be ignorant. Barthelme's stories draw their materials from the recognizable clichés and stereotypes of modern life, it's true, but his graphics often come from collagists' art books compiled by Dick Sutphen which give no indication as to their source.[7] Like any collage artist, Barthelme has been attracted by a graphic twist, or by the formal possibility of juxtaposition he might make with another object he has found. So too for his words: "realtime on-line, computer-controlled wish evaporation" is a verbal collage of words and phrases from different parts of society, not necessarily parts Barthelme would discredit, only parts which together yield components for a strikingly new and funny work of art.[8] His aim has been to create a *new* work, which exists as an object in space, not a discursive commentary on the linear elements which form it.

The best examples of Barthelme's pure collage stories are collected in *Guilty Pleasures,* as "pretexts for the pleasure of cutting up and pasting together pictures, a secret vice gone public. Guilty pleasures are the best."[9] In such works as "The Expedition" and "A Nation of Wheels" he parodies dead metaphors, but not as the story's sole point. Instead, Barthelme's graphic juxtapositions and clever captioning put life back into dead words, in an amusing way (such as placing a mammoth tire at the end of a barricaded street, and commenting, "All defenses proved penetrable"; or advising "The secret police were everywhere," as a similar tire lurks in the bushes of Edouard Manet's "The Picnic").[10] Barthelme, like Frank O'Hara, defamiliarizes objects by presenting them in unusual contexts, apart from their anaesthetizing use by social and often commercial media.[11] Whenever possible, he uses the media's own techniques, but always as an opportunity to "collage in" a more striking object of attention—such as when during a boring episode of *The Ed Sullivan Show* he substitutes something more exciting, a pornographic film spliced into the network cable by pranksters.[12] Barthelme's practice does have a moral dimension, for as Frank O'Hara says, "The slightest loss of attention leads to death."[13] But his real motive and achievement has been to replace an inferior work of art with a better one.

The writer is judged not by what he has said but by what he has made. Barthelme's constructions follow the principles of collage, and are aided by the theory of abstract expressionist art. Its canvas becomes Barthelme's page; we admire the push and pull of energies he has created on that page, by juxtaposing the words of technocrats with poets, or the inventions of Goodyear and Goodrich with the paintings of Manet. A good word-collage story is "Porcupines at the University," written for the *New Yorker* in 1970 and later collected in *Amateurs*.[14] Unlike some of the stories from *City Life* which troubled Schickel and Kazin, "Porcupines" deals with a simple and recognizable world. The university seems like an actual university, and the porcupines behave like real porcupines. Barthelme's reshaping of the familiar minority student story by changing "blacks" to "porcupines" serves as ironic commentary, and also manages to tell the story in a fresh and appealing manner. On this level his achievement is no less conventional than Bernard Malamud's in "The Jewbird," where the tired situation of a smelly old uncle living with a younger family is revitalized by casting the old man as a talking bird. In these terms, the criteria Kazin used to judge Barthelme as a bad writer can be turned around to Barthelme's benefit.

But "Porcupines at the University" does so much more. Beyond the ironic commentary is the simple fun of seeing what happens when a number of unlike things—cowboys, porcupines, academic deans—are mixed together in a closed environment (or "frame," as we should say for the collagist). And beyond any moral judgment Barthelme might make on the legitimacy of student protest versus academic resistance is his artistic achievement in holding together so many dissimilar things, so that, despite all their wild disparities, they create a model of a more coherent order than we are likely to find in the quotidian world. Barthelme's skill as a collagist makes his artifice hold together. All elements in his construction are true to their own roles. The Dean speaks in character ("'And now the purple dusk of twilight time/Steals across the meadows of my heart,' the Dean said"), and when confronted by the scout ("Porcupines! . . . Thousands and thousands of them. Three miles down the road and comin' fast!") reacts like a Dean ("Maybe they won't enroll"). Later on, the cowboys wrangling the herd act their parts, debating whether to "vamoose" or "parley" with the heavily armed Dean. How a number of independently characteristic elements can be mixed together for humor is demonstrated by Barthelme's attention to the full scene:

Meanwhile the porcupine wrangler was wrangling the porcupines across the dusty and overbuilt West.

Dust clouds, Yips. The lowing of porcupines.

"Git along theah li'l porcupines."

Here the images and even the words themselves form a verbal collage, an animated Marlboro commercial perfect to every detail, except for those madly improbable porcupines (looking like "badly engineered vacuum cleaner attachments") which nevertheless are firmly stuck in the picture. The head wrangler himself makes occasional verbal collages in his normal course of work:

"All right you porcupines step up to that yellow line."

There was no yellow line. This was just an expression the wrangler used to keep the porcupines moving. He had heard it in the Army. The damn-fool porcupines didn't know the difference.

Barthelme also allows for typical slapstick humor (often a tool of collage), moving the Muehlbach Hotel from Kansas City to New York and playing jokes with his disparate material:

He looked at the head wrangler's arm, which had a lot of little holes in it.

"Hey Griswold."

"Yeah?"

"How'd you get all them little holes in your arm?"

"You ever try to slap a brand on a porky-pine?"

Defamiliarized items from the real world mix with Barthelme's fantasies, such as when the herd of porcupines is "moving down a twelve-lane trail of silky-smooth concrete. Signs along the trail said things like 'NEXT EXIT 5 MI.' 'RADAR IN USE.' "

The Dean tries to dodge the porcupines' situation by manipulating language. He has nothing against porcupines, he implies; it's just that "We don't have *facilities* for four or five thousand porcupines." His wife suggests, "They could take Alternate Life Styles." But again it isn't Barthelme's motive to tell his readers something they already know, that in the 1960s some college administrators were callous toward minority students. Instead, he shows us things we may have forgotten: how words themselves take on bogus meanings, how certain scenes are so familiar that we no longer see them until something noteworthy is dropped in their midst. As Frank O'Hara insisted, "a painting is a sheer extension, not a window or a door; collage is as much about paper as about form . . . a sensual interest in materials comes first."[15] By emphasizing objects rather than meaning, Barthelme can have the porcupines be porcupines, cattle, and students all at the same time. In terms of metaphor, the tenor fades away and we are left with the materials of pure vehicle. The reader then participates with Barthelme in his push and pull of juxtapositions; instead of telling us something obviously apparent, he takes us through his own process of awakening and rediscovery.

Barthelme's stories which do not incorporate distinct graphic or verbal collages still rely on words and images as objects, much as they would be used by a collagist. The best examples of these are collected in *Sadness*[16] which includes stories Barthelme has identified as parts of an aborted novel,[17] and which are the closest yet he has come to social mimesis. "Critique de la Vie Quotidienne," a story completely concerned with the quotidian world, actually has the same structure as the highly experimental and almost fully abstract "Sentence" from *City Life*. Each uses overly long sentences—several pages at a time in the former, and eight full pages in the latter. Barthelme makes these long sentences bearable by the insertion of vividly interesting nouns, verbs, and gerunds; "Sentence," which is really about nothing other than a grammatical sentence working its way down one page and across to another, features a panoply of objects (a wife on her way to the shower, an FM radio playing rock music) such as would flatter the most mimetic of socially realistic stories. But Barthelme's story is not mimetic, or even referential; it is simply a sentence. "Critique" takes objects from a beleaguered husband's middle-class life and, in its second paragraph, strings them together in three interminable sentences—interminable except for their interesting profusion of objects and attitudes:

> Slumped there in your favorite chair, with your nine drinks lined up on the side table in soldierly array, and your hand never far from them, and your other hand holding on to the plump belly of the overfed child, and perhaps rocking a bit, if the chair is a rocking chair as mine was in those days, then it is true that a tiny tendril of contempt—strike that, *content*—might curl up from the storehouse where the world's content is kept, and reach into your softened brain and take hold there, persuading you that this, at last, is the fruit of all your labors, which you'd been wondering about in some such terms as, "Where is the fruit?" and so, newly cheered and warmed by this false insight, you reach out with your free hand (the one that is not clutching the nine drinks) and pat the hair of the child, and the child looks up into your face, gauging your mood as it were, and says, "Can I have a horse?," which is after all a perfectly reasonable request in some ways, but in other ways is total ruin to that state of six-o'clock equilibrium you have so painfully achieved, because it, the child's request, is of course absolutely out of the question, and so you say "No!" as forcefully as possible—a bark rather like a bite—in such a way as to put the quietus on this project, having a horse, once and for all, permanently. But, placing yourself in

the child's ragged shoes, which look more like used Brillo pads than shoes now that you regard them closely, you remember that time long ago on the other side of the Great War when you too desired a horse, and so, pulling yourself together, and putting another drink in your mouth (that makes three, I believe), you assume a thoughtful look (indeed, the same grave and thoughtful look you have been wearing all day, to confuse your enemies and armor yourself against the indifference of your friends) and begin to speak to the child softly, gently, cunningly even, explaining that the genus horse prefers the great open voids, where it can roam, and graze, and copulate with other attractive horses, to the confined space of a broke-down brownstone apartment, and that a horse if obtained would not be happy here, in the child's apartment, and does he, the child, want an unhappy horse, moping and brooding, and lying all over the double bed in the bedroom, and perhaps vomiting at intervals, and maybe even kicking down a wall or two, to express its rage? (pp. 4–5)

The motive here is not reference but readability, as the motive behind abstract expressionism is viewability. The sentence again is aware of itself, striking words and substituting others. The father's image of the horse is so vivid as to become a picture itself. What Barthelme has done is cleverly leap from object to object, from the nine drinks on the side table to the plump child to the shoes like Brillo pads to the horse, all as equally conjunctive grammatical subjects and objects, because they are essentially objects themselves which the author is stringing together in the syntax of his story. Later on, when at the end of the infamous bed-wetting episode the father complains, "Holy Hell. . . . Is there to be no end to this *family life?*" (p. 7), his exclamation is deliberately melo-dramatic. Following a page of stilted exchanges, it reads like a collaged-in comment amid the rubble of a ruined marriage and parenthood—just the posterlike quality Barthelme seeks to achieve for his socially pertinent stories. "Critique" is composed of several such posters, each a verbal set piece of recalled disasters, organized around the objects of discord. Our own memories work this way, and Barthelme's achievement is to find human relevance beyond simple mimesis.

In 1974, for an anthology edited by Rust Hills, Barthelme chose his own favorite story, "Paraguay," and revealed the reason why. "Mixing bits of this and that from various areas of life to make something that did not exist before is an oddly hopeful endeavor," Barthelme reported.

The sentence "Electrolytic jelly exhibiting a capture ratio far in excess of stand-ard is used to fix animals in place" made me very happy—perhaps in excess of its merit. But there is in the world such a thing as electrolytic jelly; the "capture ratio" comes from the jargon of sound technology; and the animals themselves are a salad of the real and the invented. The flat, almost "dead" tone paradox-ically makes possible an almost-lyricism.[18]

In an interview published that same year Barthelme added,

The point of collage is that unlike things are stuck together to make, in the best case, a new reality. This new reality, in the best case, may be or imply a comment on the other reality from which it came, and may also be much else. It's an *itself*, if it's successful: Harold Rosenberg's "anxious object," which does not know whether it's a work of art or a pile of junk.[19]

And in a 1975 symposium with William H. Gass, Grace Paley, and Walker Percy at Washington and Lee University, Barthelme brought up the subject again.

One of the funny things about experimentalism in regard to language is that most of it has not been done yet. Take *mothball* and *vagina* and put them together and see if they mean anything together; maybe you're not happy with the combination and you throw that on the floor and pick up the next two and so on. There's a lot of basic research which hasn't been done because of the enormous resources of the language and the enormous number of resonances from the past which have precluded this way of investigating language.

He then described his story "Bone Bubbles" (from *City Life*) as an example of such experiments.[20] Later in the discussion he compared the principle of collage in art with modern and contemporary modes of writing (p. 24), and as the symposium concluded, Barthelme and Gass considered the similar influences on writing of montage and collage (p. 26).

Just as film and abstract modes of art redirected the visual aesthetics of art earlier in this century, Barthelme's word-collages are changing the aesthetics of fiction. But there are sources for what Barthelme is doing: his manner of making graphic collages is partly dependent upon Max Ernst, who in turn published an entire graphic-collage novel (something Barthelme has not yet attempted) in 1934, *Une Semaine de Bonté*.[21] The seven sections of this "surrealistic novel in collage" follow the days of the week, one of the simplest patterns for narrative fiction. And the materials of Ernst's collages are likewise recognizable from the real world. But these were only his starting materials. From engravings of nineteenth-century sentimental scenes, fantasy creations of graphic artists, gargoyles, animals, and natural elements Ernst composed a narrative of objects, none referring to anything but itself. And as Barthelme proposes for his own art, Ernst's product became "an *itself*," a new reality which by its defamiliarization process threw the reality of the daily world into higher relief. Barthelme may not proceed exactly in this direction, for Ernst did not use a single word. Barthelme's goal is to create similar objects, but with the stricter discipline of using language. Applying the aesthetics of collage to the linguistic signifiers of our culture is his means of reaching this goal.

But there is a source beyond Max Ernst: the American artist, Joseph Cornell. Because Ernst's collage depends so heavily upon dynamic and kinetic juxtaposition, upon the viewer's impelled movement from one unlikely element to the next, some critics have insisted that collage is in fact a linear art. By extension, the argument could run full circle: that the elements of Barthelme's compositions are fragmentary, and that his end products do not cohere. The works of Joseph Cornell, however, are executed in the form of boxes, which contain objects more romantically suggestive (even symbolic) than comic. Dore Ashton has demonstrated how Cornell's intention derives from the romantics and symbolists, and how his assemblages are meant to suggest moments of mystical configuration, capturing magical connections within such personally familiar objects as clay pipes, stamps, and train schedules.[22] The results cannot be read linearly—the connections work only in a spatial sense.

The novelist Steve Katz has made his own Cornell-like construction from instances of the number "43," and explains the use of such petty examples of common magic (including astrology and the like): "These systems are tools useful to help you yourself arrive at a description of reality, but as soon as you depend on the system itself for the answers, start looking *at* it rather than *through* it, there begins to form a cataract of dogma over your perception of things as they are." The very zaniness of Cornell's choice of objects precludes taking them seriously for themselves; and by emphasizing the idiosyncratic in their choice, he makes their importance personal, rather than systematic. There may be real connections somewhere, beyond our reach; indeed, when things happen in coincidence, we feel happy—as Katz says, he is "grateful for a mysterious resonance that sometimes occurs and illuminates."

The practical benefit? "It does seem relaxing to find that one of these systems works for us," Katz insists, "because suddenly certain of our responsibilities for ourselves are taken off our heads for the moment, and we can give up some anxieties and get high."[23] That high, Katz shows, collapses when we respond to the system which produced it in any other than spatial fashion. Barthelme's fictions work the same way.[24] To be perceived properly, they must be read as the art not of commentary, but of collage.

Avant-garde and After

AMERICAN FICTION in the 1970s had stood at the brink of degeneration or transformation, of death or rebirth, according to which critical school one heeds. By the end of the previous decade its self-consciously problematic nature, dating back to Hawthorne's prefaces and Howells' theology of realism, clearly had reached the point of crisis. The issues were representation and mimesis—with one group of novelists and critics insisting that the true art of fiction lay in the writing, and the other more interested in what was written *about*. The division was much deeper than the earlier, nineteenth century debate between romanticism and realism, for the question ran deeper than the imaginative versus documentary approaches to one's subject. The need for subject itself was now under question. What are we, asks Ronald Sukenick in his artistically self-considered novel, *Up,* "children reading fairy tales or men trying to work out the essentials of our fate?"[1]

"It's all words and nothing but words," Sukenick's stand-in character argues, a view of fiction shared by many innovative writers of the period. Critic and novelist William H. Gass appreciates the dilemma, which raises a question never before voiced in two centuries of rabidly debated American fiction: "It seems incredible, the ease with which we sink through books quite out of sight, pass clamorous pages into soundless dreams." The challenge, which more conservative author-critics such as John Gardner and Walker Percy would not face, was abrupt and even terminal. "That novels should be made out of words, and merely words, is shocking, really," Gass admits. "It's as though you had discovered that your wife were made of rubber: the bliss of all those years, the fears . . . from sponge."[2]

Not heeding Sukenick's and Gass' advice, in a culture which had long since accepted abstraction in music, art, and poetry, invited dire consequences for fiction. By passing through language onto the projected screen of representation the narrative artist began to rely too heavily on representation's own code—in short, to do less writing and more posturing with content. "Novels are cluttered with all kinds of signals, flashing and gesturing so that the author may direct our attention to a particular configuration of character or plot in order that his work, such as it is, may be made simpler for him, and for us," novelist Gilbert Sorrentino points out.[3] Put a character in shabby clothes to show his shabby habits, and the reader will assume he's "low"; give him Vuiton luggage and we expect the best (if the worst happens, then it's great irony). "Such signals assure us that we are here, oh yes, in the world that we understand; what we 'understand' are the signals." The problem is that the writer is no longer writing, but telling the reader what he wants to hear, what he already knows. Television thrives on this principle.

"Signals are gimmicks," Sorrentino complains, for

They allow the writer to slip out from under the problems that only confrontation with his materials can solve. Novels are made of words. The difficulty in writing fiction is that the words must be composed so that they reveal the absolute reality of their prey, their subject—and at the same time, they must be in themselves real. (p. 196)

William Carlos Williams mastered this technique in poetry, where his rigorously visual imagination caught the essential design of things and reproduced not their image but their very objecthood recreated on the page. "The novel must exist outside of the life it deals with; it is not an imitation. The novel is an invention, something that is made; it is not the expression of 'self' [Romanticism]; it does not mirror reality [Realism]" (p. 196). What Sorrentino wants is not the real but "the processes of the real . . . not the meaning of life, but a revelation of its actuality" (p. 197).

Writing nonrepresentational fiction means abandoning virtually all the conventions of realistic narrative, from the simplest axioms of mimesis to the larger mythic structures underlying novelistic art, in the latter case surpassing the innovations of James Joyce, Virginia Woolf, and other Modernists who retained in their work a deep substructure of meaning. Such a step had been easier for painting, sculpture, and music, for there are no conceptual messages in daubs of paint, quantities of mass, or sounds on the tonal scale. But words are never just themselves; their referential quality invites a world of associations shared by readers, conceptual references the author might not intend and certainly cannot control. To keep the action on the page, and off the projected screen of conceptualization, became the challenge for fiction in the seventies.

The best aesthetic for deconceptualized fiction has been proposed by Ronald Sukenick in his three "Digressions" articles.[4] His first task is to challenge the exclusive legitimacy of socially realistic fiction—once just one of the things fiction could do, but for the past hundred years virtually the only thing. "The impossible situation of the realistic novel was that the better an imitation it was of 'reality' in the Aristotelian sense, the more it was an imitation of the other, Platonic sense: a shadow, a second-hand version, a counterfeit," Sukenick explains. "The more intensely the novel was 'about' life, the less it was a part of it" (*NLH,* p. 431). Fiction is no more "about" its content than music is "about" its melody—"subject matter is just one element of the composition." Composition, a criterion so rarely invoked for the study of traditional fiction, is for Sukenick a key element in the new fiction's success. Just as the abstract expressionist action painters disavowed the canvas as an illusionistic surface on which to represent and instead hailed it, with all honesty, as "an arena in which to act" (the phrase is Harold Rosenberg's), so too did Sukenick and his colleagues seize the novel as a field of action in which to play out the energy of their writing. Frank O'Hara's New York School of Poetry (closely derived from critical experience with the action painting of Jackson Pollock, Franz Kline, Willem de Kooning, and Hans Hofmann) was another model, where "The poem is not different from experience, it is more experience"—like a de Kooning canvas, a new object added to the world.

How are abstract works to be judged? By the energy and compositional integrity of their execution. That is how art and music have been criticized for centuries, while only fiction has been held to the standards of back-fence gossip or pious moralizing. Just as such open-field poetry can be traced back from Frank O'Hara to Charles Olson, Allen Ginsberg, William Carlos Williams and Walt Whitman, the new fiction finds its greatest ancestor in Henry Miller:

> Henry Miller is for American novelists what Whitman is for American poets. The source of his vitality is the current that began flowing when he reconnected our art with our experience. Experience begins with the self and Miller put the self back into fiction. For a writer the whole point of literary technique is the fullest possible release of the energy of his personality into his work, and when one comes into contact with that force, the whole superstructure that one had assumed to be the point of literature begins to burn away. (*PR,* p. 96)

But the writer's energy, so often sexual, is touchy business for the classically trained reader and critic. "The hermeneutics of the New

Criticism was, in part, a prophylaxis designed to protect life from the disruptive energy of art,'' Sukenick argues (*PR,* p. 90). His own fiction revitalizes reality (instead of copying it) by recreating its processes in an artificial, and hence humanly sympathetic, way; the world is no longer meaningless or absurd because the writer's act has made it relevant—to his own imagination and to the reader's, who shares in the fiction's making just as a viewer recreates the dance of a Jackson Pollock drip painting by following its motion on the canvas plane.

What of the writer's tools and fiction's elemental components— words—which by the reader's habit of conceptualization can break free of the fiction and bounce loose in the universe of linguistically possible associations? Here Sukenick reminds us that in fiction we are in an artistic, and not historical, world. "The words used meditatively in a literary work are not the same words used instrumentally in the world of action," he cautions. "Words in dreams do not mean the same thing as words in the newspaper." As an example, he shows how "The word *fog* in *Bleak House* does not mean the same thing as the word *fog* in the dictionary, though its meaning in *Bleak House,* once developed, could be, probably has been, added to the general sense—one sees this process on any page of the OED [Oxford English Dictionary]." Signification alone is not the final issue. "What language signifies in a literary work is different from what it signifies in its general sense, but then may be added to that sense" (*NLH,* p. 434).

Moreover, there are several strategies by which the writer can fix his or her action (and hence the reader's attention) on the page, making the words hold fast to their created image. A favorite technique is the comically overwrought metaphor, which in the very distance between its tenor and vehicle creates a mimetically unbridgeable gap, closeable only by the reader's imagination which appreciates how ridiculous the implied comparison is. In the 1960s Richard Brautigan was the master of this technique. His *Trout Fishing in America* tosses such metaphors at the reader like one-line jokes.[5] A bedridden character lies in "a tattered revolution of old blankets" (p. 8), grass turns "flat-tire brown" through the summer "and stayed that way until the rain, like a mechanic, began in the late autumn" (p. 20), and trout wait in streams "like airplane tickets" (p. 78). Because of their exotic and self-consciously fantastical nature, these phrases can only be accepted *as metaphors,* as artifacts designed by the writer not for referential value (mechanics, revolutions, and plane tickets have little to do with the action in *Trout Fishing in America*) but as objects in themselves, items crafted by the author for our imaginative delight.

Another way to bring attention to language itself is to make fun of its oddities. Donald Barthelme began his career in fiction this way, writing expanded *New Yorker* filler items such as whole stories made up in the form of *TV Guide* program notes, *Consumer Reports* product analyses, new wave Italian film scenarios, and newsmagazine stylistic redundancies.[6] His novel *Snow White*[7] includes a scene where the heroine sits down to a breakfast table stocked with her favorite cereals, "Chix, Rats, and Fear" (p. 6); a Lyndon Johnson–like leader wages "The President's War on Poetry" (p. 55). Barthelme's story "Report" draws its energy from play with engineers' language for military hardware and software. "We have rots, blights, and rusts capable of attacking [the enemy's] alphabet," they claim, plus "the deadly testicle-destroying telegram."[8] They are also at work in "the area of realtime, on-line, computer-controlled wish evaporation" to meet "the rising expectations of the world's peoples, which are as you know rising entirely too fast" (p. 54). Barthelme's latest work, collected in *Great Days,* consists of disembodied sentences, set off in dashes as the European manner, functioning as pure units of discourse passing through the universe without need of narrative situation, narrator, or even author.[9] The writer's presence is thus completely effaced, and what is left is only the words themselves.

More elaborate strategies to make language refer to itself involve the larger structure of the novel. Walter Abish uses the alphabet as his code in *Alphabetical Africa.*[10] The first chapter is titled "A," and is composed of words all beginning with that letter. The second chapter, "B," adds words beginning with that letter, and the practice is followed in ascending fashion on through the alphabet. At chapter "I" the first person narrator is introduced; other persons, places, and things await their own letter designation to appear. In terms of story, things gradually expand until by chapter "Z" anything and everything is possible. But then the book contracts, moving backwards through "Y," "X," and "W" again until we are back at "A." Old friends leave us—not by plot device, but by order of the self-conscious structure, which the reader can easily anticipate. Throughout attention is focused on language and its most elemental constituent, the letter. At each turn of the action, and at every chapter, we are reminded how artificial the entire affair has been.

Gilbert Sorrentino's novels use attention-getting structures to similarly keep the reader's attention. *The Sky Changes* and *Steelwork* are respectively notes of an automobile trip across America and memories of the author's old neighborhood in Brooklyn.[11] But the familiar, aesthetically anaesthetizing orders of time and space are discarded in favor of a more lyrical structure, in which images and their constituent words serve as links among the chronologically jumbled sections (composing in short disjunctive paragraphs is a favorite method of many recent innovators). Sorrentino's third novel, *Imaginative Qualities of Actual Things,*[12] incorporates the author in the making of his story—a technique shared with Kurt Vonnegut (*Slaughterhouse-Five*), John Barth (*Chimera*), Ronald Sukenick (*Up*), Steve Katz (*The Exagggerations of Peter Prince*), and so many other contemporary Americans that the challenge remains to make this once-startling innovation fresh and appealing. Sorrentino's strategy is to taunt himself with literary conventions that he hates and with characters he despises even more, and then use his anger and frustration to fire up his writing. Hence figures are characterized not by their puppetlike posings, but rather in their author's verbal rage. Even when speaking themselves, their remarks are subverted by the author's snide and degrading footnotes. In this way Sorrentino fulfills his own requirement, that the words capture both their subject's reality and their own.

Splendide-Hotel is Sorrentino's experiment with alphabetical structure.[13] But unlike Walter Abish's rigid technique, the letters merely serve as catalysists for verbal musings—the A's like flies, breeding in decay, the babble of B's, the "C notes" which finance Chapter Three. More provocations to write than instructions to read, the devices of *Splendide-Hotel* nevertheless remind the reader that this novel springs from the artist's play with words, not from representational notions from the real world.

The most exhaustive exercise with self-apparent form is Sorrentino's fourth and by far longest novel, *Mulligan Stew.*[14] Written in the manner of Flann O'Brien's 1939 classic *At Swim-Two-Birds* (one of the few novels praised by James Joyce), Sorrentino's book is the complete artist's workshop. A story begins, but soon breaks away to its author-character's notebooks, scrapbooks, correspondence, and other jottings of daily life—all documentary material bearing equal weight with his story. Then his characters begin keeping diaries of their life apart from the story, as actors in a repertory they sometimes despise. In their off hours, rummaging about the author's stage set, they find other books (sometimes listed, other times quoted) and evidence of other fictions taking place in adjacent rooms, much as life itself goes on in all simultaneity. *Mulligan Stew* proceeds by using each of these devices several times over, until by the end, when the character-novelist's book is done, we have seen the full history of its composition. Whatever illusions there are, we have been witness to their making.

Graphic design is another favorite device to keep the reader's attention on the page. Raymond Federman's *Double or Nothing* was printed as a photographed typescript because its form is modelled upon a secretary's typewriter game, in which each page of the evolving story is typed up in some graphic form: Christmas tree, pyramid, hourglass, and so forth.[15] On certain pages the reader must rotate the book, for the page is typed in a circle; another page is backwards, and can be read only in a mirror. Reading *Double or Nothing* is not a sedentary affair. Ronald Sukenick's *Out* uses the physical design of the book and the reader's act of reading it for physical effect.[16] Concerned with the forward momentum of his story, Sukenick has often used deliberately run-on sentences and lack of punctuation to achieve a syncopated "stumbling forward" effect, impelling the reader onward through his prose. *Out* uses this and more concrete methods to speed up the reading process, numbering its chapters backward from ten, having each chapter characterized by block paragraphs with steadily decreasing numbers of lines and increasing units of space (9-1, 8-2, 7-3, 6-4, and so forth) until by chapter one there is but one line of print for every nine lines of space. The result is that the reader moves faster and faster, flipping pages with accelerating speed until by chapter zero the book disappears into blank space.

Graphic form can also be a discipline, much like a sonnet structure, forcing the writer into fresher combinations of words and images. In Raymond Federman's second novel, *Take It or Leave It,* his protagonist (a young French immigrant drafted into the American Army) earns money writing torrid "French love letters" for his barracks mates.[17] Reproduced in typescript, we see unthinkably bizarre combinations of phraseology, exotic images, and tangled conceits, delivered in a bombastic and overblown parody of purple prose. A closer look shows that right and left margins are perfectly justified: no hyphenations, no ragged edges, no blank spaces. The author has composed and recomposed each line until it equalled sixty characters, seaching for right-numbered synonyms until each line turned out even. Without this self-imposed discipline the comedy of his language might never have been achieved. And without its typescript form, the technique of highly artificial language would not be so apparent to the reader.

The most successfully innovative work, free of gimmicks and purely mechanical devices, has been done by Clarence Major. His *Reflex and Bone Structure* takes place almost entirely within the realm of language, as its author self-consciously creates the story as a pondered detective novel; its characters develop within their own mental associations of words and images, and the action itself occurs with the placing of words on a page.[18] Stimuli from television and records are as real as, even more real than events in everyday life, for the characters exist within their hyper-suggestive imaginations (as projections of the author's own imagination as he sifts through the materials of his story). Phrases from life and from the TV screen merge, establishing the story's action in the images and their component words:

> We're in bed watching the late movie. It's 1938. *A Slight Case of Murder.* Edward G. Robinson and Jane Bryan.
>
> I go into the bathroom to pee. Finished, I took at my aging face. Little Caesar. I wink at him in the mirror. He winks back.
>
> I'm back in bed. The late late show comes on. It's 1923. *The Bright Shawl.* Dorothy Gish, Mary Astor. I'm taking Mary Astor home in a yellow taxi. Dorothy Gish is jealous. (p. 3)

Time in "real life" yields to the artificial, humanly created time of moving pictures; the characters likewise exist in fully artificial images. At a second remove from the film's story, Major's narrative requires no illusions, yet functions with the full power of narrative's own conventions. Other times, as in the paintings of René Magritte, Major slips deliberately surreal images into otherwise realistic scenes (a rubber plant dries the dishes, the TV slushes back and forth), reminding the reader that for all the comfortable associations with reality this is still an artificially constructed work. Scenes are replayed according to different perspectives, different characters' imaginations. Most of all, the action is happening on the page, as the author thinks back on the story he's been constructing:

> I am standing behind Cora. She is wearing a black nightgown. The backs of her legs are lovely. I love her. The word standing allows me to watch like this. The word nightgown is what she is wearing. The nightgown itself is in her drawer with her panties. The word Cora is wearing the word nightgown. I watch the sentence: The backs of her legs are lovely. (p. 74)

Major's *Emergency Exit* extends the techniques of his previous novel to effectively deconceptualize language itself, so that the book's action takes place not only on the page but within the letters of the words (without conceptual references) themselves.[19] The "story" is disturbingly conventional, a love triangle among ghetto and suburbanized black characters in present-day Connecticut. But Major has found several ways to keep the story from turning into social realism. As in *Reflex,* images are culled from American popular culture—movies, records, and folk mores. At first seemingly used as shorthand symbols for attitudes and actions, they soon become objects in themselves (bibliographies, telephone-book pages) to be admired for their artifice. A mood emerges from them quite independently of the narrative story line, and as a result that story line becomes less important to the reader. Attention has been focused on the writing and on the words.

121

Secondly, and most effectively, Major has found a way to make potential linguistic references point inward toward his own novel rather than outward to the world. The technique is simple, even elemental. After the barest introduction in which the author sketches out his concerns in writing this novel, component sections begin to appear in apparently random order. Some consist of simple sentences—pure descriptions which, because we do not yet know their context, are interesting because of their words alone. In time, these words and phrases will be developed into larger images, which recur as verbal pictures; soon the reader is accustomed to the presence of a lighthouse, a beach, a peculiar quality of sun and sky, and so forth. But the scene has yet to be animated. Before that come component paragraphs, prose poems in which disembodied actions dance before us in purely linguistic delight. Then there are vignettes: a visiting African professor struggling amid the junk and clutter of an American supermarket, a young black college girl exploring her emerging sexuality, and still others which only later will connect with the larger text. Finally, every so often Major dips back into his narrative line, the story of Al and Julie and her family. But the story grows not simply through its narrative accumulations, but more by virtue of its inward references to words from the earlier independent sentences, paragraphs, and vignettes. When Al and Julie meet by the lighthouse, we think not of all the lighthouses we may have seen in our own world, but of the shadowy figure which appeared in Julie's dream (an earlier vignette), the lighthouse in the paragraph prose poem we read before, and ultimately the word "lighthouse" as Major established it in one of his curious, attention-riveting sentences near the start of the book. Hence language which all too dangerously can refer outward here leads inward, toward the author's own created structure. For all practical purposes, language has been deconceptualized. All references are contained within the novel's own world.

Clarence Major's innovations have made a fully nonrepresentational fiction possible. Such a radical aesthetic makes for an entirely new kind of fiction, much as visual art was reinvented by the cubists in the first decade of this century and carried to its logical and technical extreme by the abstract expressionists forty years later. Certain critics have feared that the loss of representation means the loss of meaning, that "action painting in words" would mean little more than the typescripts of monkeys playing at the keys. Raymond Federman clarifies the issue in his critical anthology, *Surfiction*.[20] "To write," he argues, "is to *produce* meaning, and not *reproduce* a pre-existing meaning" (p. 8). Fiction itself is an autonomous reality. The new conventions follow in kind: reading must become a more energetic act, a participation in the process of fictional creation; no bogus order may be imposed on its events—things transpire by digression, or as Ronald Sukenick puts it, "happen to happen," like jazz; meaning itself will not preexist the fiction but be created in it. Fiction, like a poem, will not mean, but be.

Critical opposition to the deconceptualization of language in fiction has been substantial. Older spokesmen, such as Alfred Kazin and Nathan Scott, have insisted that the true matter of fiction is story, and that "novelist" is synonymous with "storyteller." Younger conservative critics, especially John Gardner and Gerald Graff, have felt the innovationists were abandoning not only the entertainments of story but the moral responsibilities of myth. Fiction should tell us how to live, Gardner argues in *On Moral Fiction,* and he means it most literally: God prescribes, heroes enact, and poets record.[21] Unwilling to admit that action painting in words enacts the artist-writer's own experience as an epitome of imaginative life, Gardner insists that fiction follow the universal code of myth, ignoring the fact that once used self-consciously such myths can never duplicate their original function.

A more formidable charge against recent American innovations is that they lack substance and appeal for the reader, that the author's self-absorption in his or her work excludes the reader by a strategy more effective than the most troubling obscurantism of the moderns. One solution has been for the writers to physically and imaginatively engage the reader in creating their fictions, whether by book design, acrobatics of metaphor, or other cooperative gestures of style. But narcissism is a serious threat to the reader's interest when there is nothing in the writing itself with which to identify.

Can innovative fiction address the world and its problems, yet remain free of the limiting conventions of realism? Following the achievements of the avant-garde, can there still be fiction with feeling? A newly emergent group of writers in the late 1970s has defined itself in response to these problems. Best characterized as the authors of "bubble gum fiction" (as "bubble gum music" of the last decade was an answer to the abrasiveness and stridency of the period's heavier rock), William Kotzwinkle, Tom Robbins, Rob Swigart, and Gerald Rosen have tried to write a socially responsive fiction which does not sacrifice the aesthetic gains of the great sixties innovators. The breakthrough work was William Kotzwinkle's *The Fan Man,* published as a paperback original (like most bubble gum fiction) in 1974.[22] Pure writing, placed in a social context, becomes pure speaking, and *The Fan Man* is a tour de force of the human voice. The speaker throughout is Horse Badorties, burnt-out sixties freak, whose running monologue dictated into an ever-present tape recorder is a living record of his life. Even walking down the street becomes an adventure: "The Plan is now formulated on my Horse Badorties tape recorder. Later on, when I have forgotten who I am, I can always turn on the tape recorder and find out that I am Horse Badorties, going to Chinatown. And now, man, I must get out of this doorway and walk along the street" (p. 23).

The pure human voice, engaged in no other activity than simply talking (often with no real reference other than itself), becomes Kotzwinkle's form of gossip-free fiction. The materials of its artifice are not persons, places, and things, but rather adjectives, verbs, and nouns—syntax is a subject worthy of its own narrative. "The rent will be high but it's not so bad if you don't pay it," Horse reflects (p. 11). What was once the advertising slogan of Household Finance is twisted into a work of verbal art: "easy terms borrow needlessly when you must" (p. 116). An entire chapter, "It's Dorky Day Again," is narrated in and about the single word of Horse's mantra, chanted endlessly amidst the actions of two counterposed subplots, making of silence a fuctional object. Horse Badorties is an improvisational artist, a *bricoleur,* who makes do with the materials at hand—electric cord for a belt, earflap hat to drown out Latin pachanga music—and wings his way through experiences and sentences. His apartment, like his syntax, is a mess. "Listen, Baby," he tells one of his ever-present fifteen-year-old girl friends, "you can take a bath here. I'll scrub your back. The tub is around here someplace . . . " (p. 150). He stumbles through life like he stumbles through his sentences, and by the second chapter we can easily identify his character by just a few words ("Horse Badorties here, man. Hey, man, what planet am I on?"). But Horse's language has preceded any of his adventures, and those adventures are interesting only because we've first come to know his manner of speech. Despite all its references to Horse Badorties' world, *The Fan Man* is primarily a novel of language.

The first underground classic of bubble gum fiction is Tom Robbins' *Another Roadside Attraction,* published in 1971 but marketed by word-of-mouth among college and counterculture readerships in the mid-seventies.[23] Robbins, a former student of religion and practicing art critic, brings a wealth of philosophical interest to the writing of this novel. He feels that the excessive rationalization of Western culture since Descartes has severed man from his roots in nature. Organized religion has in like manner become more of a tool of logic and control than of spirit. Robbins' heroine, Amanda, would reconnect mankind with the benign chaos of the natural world, substituting magic for logic, style for substance, and poetry for the analytical measure of authority. But to show the reader how magical, suprarational connections work, to involve the reader in recomposing the world according to their wacky structures, Robbins describes each point of action with a mind-bending metaphor or simile, often run to considerable length:

Man, Purcell has a grin like the beer barrel polka. A ding-dong daddy grin. A Brooklyn Dodger grin. A grin you would wear to a Polish wedding. His smile walks in in woolly socks and suspenders and asks to borrow the funny papers. You could trap rabbits with it. Teeth line up inside it like cartridges in a Mexican bandit's gunbelt. It is the skunk in his rosebush, the crack in his cathedral. (p. 89)

Other examples are about language itself ("The 'but' that crouched like a sailor there in the doorway of his second sentence did not in any way tie his first remark to his second one. It was a 'but' more ornamental than conjunctional") (p. 231). At his best, Robbins gives the reader one metaphor, then asks cooperation in tying a second one to it, as in "It was a peekaboo summer. The sun was in and out like Mickey Rooney" (p. 235).

Robbins is a master of plain American speech, as simple as hot dogs, baseball, apple pies, and Chevrolet, and his greatest trick is to use its flat style to defuse the most sacred objects. The plot of his novel is most appealing precisely because of this subverting style, as when Amanda's friend bodysnatches the corpse of Christ for a roadside zoo:

The Second Coming did not quite come off as advertised. The heavens opened, sure enough, but only to let a fine pearly rain streak through to spray the valley. Instead of celestial choirs, there were trucks snorting on the Freeway. Instead of Gabriel's trumpet there was John Paul Ziller's flute. Jesus himself showed up disguised as a pop art sculpture, caked with plaster from head to toe. And contrary to advance publicity, he was in no better shape upon his return than he was at his departure. He was, in fact, dead as a boot. (p. 264)

The point of *Another Roadside Attraction* is the reinvention (through perception) of reality, a revitalization of life which logic and authority have dulled beyond appreciation. But as a message, it is not simply preached or discussed. Instead, Robbins makes the actual reading of his novel an experience in the stylistic transformation he has in mind. A successful reading of his book makes the reader an initiate, for he or she has performed the same mental tricks, the same imaginative acrobatics, as have the fictional characters in Robbins' story.

Tom Robbins' second novel, *Even Cowgirls Get the Blues,* extends both technique and belief from the earlier book.[24] Here the heroine is Sissy Hankshaw, whose physical deformity (giant thumbs) is transformed into a positive asset: hitchhiking. "Freedom of movement" becomes her credo, and Robbins' too (to expound upon it, he puts himself into the novel as a clinical psychiatrist). As Sissy uses her magic to travel great distances, so does Robbins carry the reader across great expanses of metaphorical connections, as in *Another Roadside Attraction.* But now Robbins makes his metaphors even more kinesthetic, so that every scene is put into motion; the book must be read with body English. A hermit's lodge on a Dakota butte may be static in itself, but once within the author's language it becomes a kaleidoscope of verbal action: "The shack was strategically erected at the narrow entrance to the valley, which, with a creek as its racing stripe, totalled out against the base of the tunnel-filled knoll" (p. 196).

Motion and change, by now familiar to the reader who has been practicing them in every sentence, are explained as recent developments in human evolution, spurred on as a relief from the oppressive limits of analytical reason. "By pushing it, goosing it along whenever possible," Robbins explains, "we may speed up the process, the process by which the need for playfulness and liberty becomes stronger than the need for comfort and security" (p. 206). Repeating his message from the first novel, Robbins adds that "the vagrancies and violence of nature must be brought back into the foreground of social and political consciousness, that they have got to be embraced in any meaningful psychic renewal." The writing of his novels, and the new style of imagination they speak to (Robbins' following is almost entirely countercultural), indicate that such change may already be under way.

Rob Swigart, author of *Little America, A. K. A./A Cosmic Fable,* and *The Time Trip,* follows Robbins' magical use of language and view of life by adding a genius for developing multiple plots.[25] Things hang together in ways far beyond our limited vision, Swigart insists, and to the wide-reaching metaphor he adds the delight of interconnecting actions. Chapters are linked by key words hopscotching from one plot to another; key events in one trigger mechanisms worlds away. These connections finally celebrate only their own artifice. Ultimate meanings are less important than the simple joy in learning how one fragment can trip another, like a Rube Goldberg invention, so in this sense bubble gum fiction matures into pin ball fiction.

The most serious writer of this style is Gerald Rosen. His first novel, *Blues for a Dying Nation,* uses language, metaphor, and plot complication—all in their self-apparent artifice—to create an image of Vietnamized America.[26] Virtually every truth we learned from those years—how antiguerilla warfare invents its own enemy, how technology and linguistics create their own level of reality in warfare, how armies destroy villages in order to save them, how language itself is debased—is suggested by the artifices in Rosen's book. As a way of keeping his story clear of social reality, yet to remind the reader how similarly absurd events actually transpired in the American 1960s, Rosen inserts occasional newspaper clippings. The resulting collage of real world and imaginary story form a full testament, more vital than a similar documentary effort might be to these years in America's life.

Rosen's second novel, *The Carmen Miranda Memorial Flagpole,* is built on the positive energy of the 1960s and is thus a much more cheerful book.[27] Even with unpleasant subjects, his language manages to celebrate its artifice with comedy and a sense of the ridiculous, as for an obnoxious housewife who has "an expression on her face . . . so sour that I figure either she's in great physical pain or else she has swallowed a tape deck that's playing country and western music and she can't turn it off" (p. 129). The book itself is propelled by a series of one-line jokes ("the only art form we had in the Bronx"), which keeps the action moving as fast and as frantic as in a stand-up comedian's patter. The story concerns two brothers driving cross-country from New York to California, performing corny routines all the way (Knute Rockne movies for Notre Dame, Carl Sandburg poems in Chicago, a one-man rendition of Martha and the Vandellas' "Heat Wave" at the Grand Canyon to scare off some annoying tourists).

Rosen, like his bubble gum colleagues, has a serious message to deliver. But he makes that message part of the novel's form, not content. The narrator has a brother (though it may only be part of his split personality, or one of his creative projections, as the "Psychiatric Introduction" suggests) who is a bubble gum fictionist himself. This brother has written a novel about "The Planet Opteema," an imaginatively created world which can replace the "majority hallucination" we otherwise accept as mundane reality. The brother's novel fails, however, and we have a doubly suspicious view of it because our narrator is a certified public accountant, straight-arrow square. Hence the transformational possibilities of fiction, plus the tension between that urge and the quotidian realities of life, are incorporated within Rosen's artifice.

Dr. Ebenezer's Book & Liquor Store is Rosen's metaphor for art's healing influence on life.[28] Books and booze are the elemental aesthetic which makes things other than they are, better than they might presently be, if only for a time. Again, language animates the novel's action, just as "a good rap" owes its success as much to the manner of telling as to the matter of what is told. And as Rob Swigart quotes Werner Heisenberg's Uncertainty Principle in the epigraph to *A.K.A.* to show how even the hard rock reality of physical science supports his relativistic theme, Rosen begins *Dr. Ebenezer* with two reminders from Niels Bohr:

"However contrasting phenomena may at first sight appear, it must be realized that they are complementary," and "There are things that are so serious you can only joke about them." The latter, of course, is an example of how the Principle of Complementarity functions in everyday life. But so much of the world resists this postmodern vision. Rosen articulates a generally held belief of the bubble gum fictionists when he blames male authority for fouling up the processes of life. His protagonist, Dr. Ebenezer, suffers from this very syndrome: a dropout from university teaching and the atomic energy program (where he helped invent the Bomb), he blames himself (the reductio ad absurdum of analytical responsibility) for the atomic holocaust in Japan and for the whole direction the uglier aspects of postwar culture have taken. A false aesthetic tempts him: Treena, whose very presence on the page invites a sensual riot of sounds, smells, and motions. Ideas, however, exist only to be outgrown. Dr. Ebenezer's hard learned lesson is that our greatness is measured only by what we can discard, by what we can outgrow. His journey is toward essentials, in his own life and in what he can offer to others. A dispenser of aesthetic condiments, he finally learns how to make his own life into a work of art—something lived, not bought. In this manner *Dr. Ebenezer's Book & Liquor Store* is a profoundly affirmative work, whose theme and technique reflect the aesthetic beliefs of fiction grown past its representational stage.

The struggle of contemporary fiction has been invigorated by the persistence of its opposition. Without the contrary voices of Alfred Kazin, Nathan Scott, John Gardner, and Gerald Graff, the innovations of Ronald Sukenick, Clarence Major, Gerald Rosen, and their colleagues would not stand out in such clear relief. But since truly self-examined fiction began with Nathaniel Hawthorne's prefaces, American novelists have thrived on the critical problems in their own work. Perhaps because America itself was from the start such an idealistic and reasoned experiment in civic problematics, the artifices of fictional art have proven to be our aesthetic specialty. American fiction has never taken itself for granted, which is why it has contributed so much to the development of fiction from Hawthorne's day to the present.

CHAPTER ONE

1. Newton Arvin, *Hawthorne* (Boston: Little, Brown, 1929), p. 192.

2. E. P. Whipple, "The House of the Seven Gables and Twice Told Tales," *Graham's Magazine,* 28 (1851), 467; E. A. Duyckinck, "The House of the Seven Gables," *The Literary World,* 8 (1851), 334.

3. The criticism of the ending is summarized by Francis Joseph Battaglia, "The House of the Seven Gables: New Light on Old Problems," PMLA, 82 (1967), 579-90.

4. *The Centenary Edition of the Works of Nathaniel Hawthorne,* ed. William Charvat, et al. (Columbus: Ohio State Univ. Press, 1962-), II, 213. Subsequent references will be to this edition.

5. Melvin Askew, "Hawthorne, The Fall, and the Psychology of Maturity," *American Literature,* 34 (1962), 335-43; Leonard J. Fick, *The Light Beyond: A Study of Hawthorne's Theology* (Westminster, Md.: Newman Press, 1955); Leo B. Levy, "The Marble Faun: Hawthorne's Landscape of the Fall," *American Literature,* 42 (1970), 139-56; Gary J. Scrimgeour, *"The Marble Faun*: Hawthorne's Faery Land," *American Literature,* 36 (1964), 271-87; Dorothy Waples, "Suggestions for Interpreting *The Marble Faun,"* *American Literature,* 13 (1941), 224-39.

6. Millicent Bell, *Hawthorne's View of the Artist* (New York: SUNY Press, 1962), p. 19; F. I. Carpenter, "Puritans Preferred Blondes: The Heroines of Melville and Hawthorne," *New England Quarterly,* 9 (1936), 226; Barris Mills, "Hawthorne and Puritanism," *New England Quarterly,* 21 (1948), 98; Richard D. Rust, "Character Change and Development in the Major Novels of Nathaniel Hawthorne," Diss. Univ. of Wisconsin 1966, p. 252.

7. Letter to James T. Fields, quoted in *Yesterdays with Authors* (Boston: J. R. Osgood, 1872), p. 51. All letters quoted from this volume have been checked against their originals in the Hawthorne-Fields Letterbook, Houghton Library, Harvard University.

8. E. P. Whipple, "The Scarlet Letter," *Graham's Magazine,* 36 (1850), 345-46.

9. *Yesterdays,* p. 109.

10. *Yesterdays,* p. 56.

11. Letter to James T. Fields in the private collection of Prof. Norman Holmes Pearson. Quoted by permission.

12. Letter to Everet A. Duyckinck, 27 Apr. 1851. MS, Duyckinck Collection, New York Public Library.

13. Letter of James T. Fields to Everet A. Duyckinck, 10 Dec. 1850. MS, Duyckinck Collection, New York Public Library.

14. Cited in note 2.

15. *Yesterdays,* p. 58.

CHAPTER TWO

1. Everett Carter, *Howells and the Age of Realism* (Philadelphia: Lippincott, 1954), pp. 104, 202–3; Gordon S. Haight, "Realism Defined: William Dean Howells," in *The Literary History of the United States,* ed. Robert E. Spiller, et al., 3d ed., rev. (New York: Macmillan, 1963), II, 889; Rudolph and Clara Kirk, *William Dean Howells: Representative Selections* (New York: Hill and Wang, 1950), pp. lxx, lxxiv n. 200; Rudolph and Clara Kirk, *William Dean Howells* (New York: Twayne, 1962), p. 71; Jay Martin, *Harvests of Change* (Englewood Cliffs, N.J.: Prentice-Hall, 1967), pp. 38–41; H. Wayne Morgan, *American Writers in Rebellion* (New York: Hill and Wang, 1965), p. 46; Larzer Ziff, *The American 1890's* (New York: Viking, 1966), p. 38.

2. William M. Gibson, "Materials and Form in Howells' First Novels," *American Literature,* 19 (May 1947), 158–66; Clara M. Kirk, "Reality and Actuality in the March Family Narratives of W. D. Howells," PMLA, 74 (1959), 137–52; John K. Reeves, "The Limited Realism of Howells' *Their Wedding Journey,*" PMLA, 77 (1962), 617–28; John K. Reeves, "The Way of a Realist: A Study of Howells' Use of the Saratoga Scene," PMLA, 45 (1950), 1035–52. Reeves has also edited the *CEAA* text of *Their Wedding Journey* for Indiana University Press (Bloomington, 1968), the Introduction to which synthesizes his own earlier work. An exception to the biographical approach is found in Marion W. Cumpanio, "The Dark Side of *Their Wedding Journey,*" *American Literature,* 40 (1969), 472–86.

3. Edwin H. Cady, *The Road to Realism* (Syracuse, N.Y.: Syracuse Univ. Press, 1956), p. 159.

4. W. D. Howells, *Their Wedding Journey* (Boston: Osgood, 1872). All quotes are taken from this first edition.

5. Olov W. Fryckstedt, *In Quest of America: A Study of Howells' Early Development as a Writer* (Cambridge: Harvard Univ. Press, 1958), p. 108.

6. George Arms, "Howells' New York Novel: Comedy and Belief," *New England Quarterly,* 21 (1948), 317; George N. Bennett, *William Dean Howells, the Development of a Novelist* (Norman: Univ. of Oklahoma Press, 1959), pp. 188–90; Carter, pp. 202, 206; Fryckstedt, pp. 252–53; Kirk and Kirk, *William Dean Howells,* p. 116; Clara M. Kirk, *W. D. Howells and Art in His Time* (New Brunswick, N.J.: Rutgers Univ. Press, 1965), p. 130.

7. W. D. Howells, *A Hazard of New Fortunes,* 2 vols. (New York: Harper and Brothers, 1890). All quotes are taken from this first edition.

8. Robert Lee Hough, *The Quiet Rebel: William Dean Howells as Social Commentator* (Lincoln: Univ. of Nebraska Press, 1959), pp. 40–42.

9. Hough refers to Howells' "An East Side Ramble," which contains perceptions similar to those of the narrator cited here.

10. Arms, pp. 322–23.

11. Hough, p. 55.

12. Hough, p. 52.

13. George C. Carrington, Jr., *The Immense Complex Journey: The World and Art of William Dean Howells* (Columbus: Ohio State Univ. Press, 1966), p. 139.

14. Clara M. Kirk, in her PMLA study (p. 139), incorrectly numbers Basil's first-person narratives as three, forgetting to count *An Open-Eyed Conspiracy.*

15. W. D. Howells, *The Shadow of a Dream* (New York: Harper and Brothers, 1890). All quotes are from this first edition.

16. Serialized respectively in *Harper's Monthly* (Nov. 1897) and *Scribner's* (Mar., Apr. 1895). Collected in *A Pair of Patient Lovers* (New York; Harper and Brothers, 1901). All quotes are from the first edition of this collection.

17. W. D. Howells, *An Open-Eyed Conspiracy* (New York: Harper and Brothers, 1897). All quotes are from this first edition.

18. Kirk, PMLA, p. 152.

19. Cited in note 2.

20. W. D. Howells, "Bibliography," *A Hazard of New Fortunes* (New York: Harper and Brothers, 1911), p. vi.

21. Ibid., p. viii.

22. Ibid.

23. Frank Norris, *Responsibilities of the Novelist* (New York: Doubleday, Page, 1903), pp. 30–31.

CHAPTER THREE

1. Malcolm Cowley, "Naturalism in American Literature," *Evolutionary Thought in America,* ed. Stow Persons (New Haven: Yale Univ. Press, 1950), p. 307.

2. Lars Ahnebrink, *The Beginnings of Naturalism in American Fiction* (Cambridge: Harvard Univ. Press, 1950), p. 53.

3. Donald Pizer, *Realism and Naturalism in Nineteenth-Century American Literature* (Carbondale: Southern Illinois Univ. Press, 1966), quoting Perry on p. 57.

4. Pizer, p. 69.

5. Pizer, p. 90.

6. Pizer, quoting from *Crumbling Idols,* p. 93.

7. Vernon Louis Parrington, *The Beginnings of Critical Realism in America,* Vol. III of *Main Currents in American Thought* (New York: Harcourt, Brace and World, 1930), p. 288; Ahnebrink, p. 5: "The settlers were in the grip of a complex of forces . . . which gouged them from all sides."

8. Clarence Gohdes, *The Literature of the American People* (New York: Appleton-Century-Crofts, 1951), p. 654.

9. Marie Fletcher, "The Southern Woman in the Fiction of Kate Chopin," *Louisiana History,* 7 (1966), 117–32; Per E. Seyersted, "Kate Chopin: An Important St. Louis Writer Reconsidered," *Missouri Historical Society Bulletin,* 19 (1963), pp. 89–114; Anonymous note, "Missouri Miniatures: Kate Chopin," *Missouri Historical Review* (1944), pp. 207–8. Seyersted's work was eventually expanded as *Kate Chopin: A Critical Biography* (Baton Rouge: Louisiana State Univ. Press, 1969).

10. Kenneth Elbe, "A Forgotten Novel: Kate Chopin's *The Awakening," Western Humanities Review,* 10 (1956), pp. 261–69; Robert Cantwell, "*The Awakening," Georgia Review,* 10 (1956), pp. 489–94.

11. New York: Viking, 1966, pp. 296–305.

12. *The New Republic,* 155, 3 Dec. 1966, pp. 22, 37–38.

13. Kate Chopin, *The Awakening* (New York: Putnam Capricorn paperback, 1965), p. 3. All further quotes will be taken from this edition, which is a photocopy of the original 1899 Chicago edition.

14. Daniel S. Rankin, *Kate Chopin and Her Creole Stories,* Diss. Univ. of Pennsylvania (University Park, Pennsylvania, 1932).

CHAPTER FOUR

1. F. Scott Fitzgerald, *This Side of Paradise* (New York: Charles Scribner's Sons, 1920). Subsequent quotes are from this edition. The historical structure for this reading is provided by Fitzgerald's major biographers, and critically by James E. Miller, Jr., in his two analytical studies, *The Fictional Technique of F. Scott Fitzgerald* (The Hague: Nijhoff, 1957) and *F. Scott Fitzgerald: His Art and His Technique* (New York: New York Univ. Press, 1964).

2. F. Scott Fitzgerald, *The Great Gatsby* (New York: Charles Scribner's Sons, 1925). Subsequent quotes are from this edition.

CHAPTER FIVE

1. Michael Millgate, *The Achievement of William Faulkner* (London: Constable, 1966), p. 270. This quote comes from a letter written in 1948 by Faulkner to Malcolm Cowley. Millgate, on pp. 259-65 and pp. 270-75, emphasizes Faulkner's care with his short story collections. He does not, however, see the need to discover the underlying unity of the *KG* collection, preferring to read it as a series of unsuccessful Gavin Stevens stories.

2. Millgate, pp. 47, 270.

3. Nelson Algren, *New York Times,* 6 Nov. 1949, 4; Warren Beck, *Chicago Sunday Tribune,* 13 Nov. 1949, 3; Malcolm Cowley, *New York Herald Tribune Book Review,* 6 Nov. 1949, 7; Irving Howe, *Nation,* 169 (1949), 473; Howard Mumford Jones, *Saturday Review of Literature,* 32 (1949), 17; Edmund Wilson, *New Yorker,* 25 (1949), 58.

4. Maurice Beebe's checklist in *Modern Fiction Studies,* 13 (1967), overestimates the contribution of the two critics who did write on *KG.* Millgate's study is five pages, not ten pages, and Vickery's contribution would be more properly described as passim. One later positive study of the title story alone is Mary M. Dunlap's "William Faulkner's 'Knight's Gambit' and Gavin Stevens," *Mississippi Quarterly,* 22 (1969), 190-206.

5. All quotations from *Knight's Gambit* are taken from the first edition published in New York by Random House in 1949.

6. James Meriwether, *The Literary Career of William Faulkner* (Princton: Princeton Univ. Library, 1961), pp. 168, 175.

7. Millgate, p. 47.

8. Meriwether, p. 162.

9. Meriwether, pp. 33-34.

10. Millgate, on p. 270, describes the "overt presence of a narrator, Chick Mallison." This is incorrect. The events of the story, including the action of the boy, are described by a third person narrator. At best, Mallison is the primary "reflector" of the action; but he does not narrate the story himself.

11. Charles H. Nilon, *Faulkner and the Negro* (New York: Citadel, 1965), pp. 73-92.

12. Cleanth Brooks, *William Faulkner: The Yoknapatawpha Country* (New Haven: Yale Univ. Press, 1963), pp. 297-98. Brooks demonstrates at many points in this volume that one of Faulkner's most enduring themes is that of community. But like most critics, he does not treat *Knight's Gambit* as pertinent; the collection is generally disregarded here and in his sequel study, *William Faulkner: Toward Yoknapatawpha and Beyond* (New Haven: Yale Univ. Press, 1978).

CHAPTER SIX

1. Robert A. Bone, *The Negro Novel in America,* rev. ed. (New Haven: Yale Univ. Press, 1965), pp. 178-79; Walter B. Rideout, *The Radical Novel in the United States* (Cambridge: Harvard Univ. Press, 1956), p. 263; Chester E. Eisinger, *Fiction of the Forties* (Chicago: Univ. of Chicago Press, 1963), p. 70.

2. Eisinger, *Fiction of the Forties,* p. 70.

3. The first group has been described by Jerome Klinkowitz, James Giles, and John T. O'Brien, "The Willard Motley Papers at the University of Wisconsin," *Resources for American Literary Study,* 2 (1972), 218-73. The second group is housed presently in the Swen Franklin Parson Library, Northern Illinois Univ., DeKalb, by agreement with the estate of Willard Motley, and has been described by Craig Abbott and Kay Van Mol, "The

Willard Motley Papers at Northern Illinois University," *Resources for American Literary Study,* 7 (1977), 3-26.

4. Motley's undated notes prefacing a file of his papers at the University of Wisconsin–Madison, quoted with the consent of Felix Pollak, curator of rare books and manuscripts. All of the previously unpublished writings of Willard Motley are published by permission of the estate of Willard Motley, Frederica Westbrooke, administratrix.

5. Victor B. Klefbeck to Motley, 9 Apr. 1938, Willard Motley Papers, Northern Illinois Univ., DeKalb. Klefbeck was editor of *Outdoors.*

6. Motley's undated notes (see note 4 above).

7. Theodore M. Purdy, "Editing Willard Motley's *Knock on Any Door,*" paper delivered at "Editors and Editing," a symposium held at the PEN American Center, New York University, 10 Feb. 1970.

8. Purdy to Motley, 1 June 1946; at DeKalb.

9. Motley to Rapport, 29 Nov. 1946 (carbon TL); at DeKalb.

10. Rapport to Motley, 12 Dec. 1946; at DeKalb.

11. Purdy to Motley, 26 Aug. 1946; at DeKalb.

12. From the unpublished manuscript; at DeKalb.

13. Lee's review appeared in the *New York Times,* 4 May 1947, p. 3. Motley to Purdy, 1 May 1947 (carbon TL); at DeKalb.

14. Motley to Purdy, n.d. (carbon TL); at DeKalb.

CHAPTER SEVEN

1. New York: Alfred A. Knopf, 1959.
2. New York: Alfred A. Knopf, 1960.
3. New York: Alfred A. Knopf, 1965.
4. New York: Alfred A. Knopf, 1975.
5. New York: Alfred A. Knopf, 1963.
6. New York: Alfred A. Knopf, 1968.
7. New York: Alfred A. Knopf, 1962.
8. New York: Alfred A. Knopf, 1969.
9. New York: Alfred A. Knopf, 1970.
10. New York: Alfred A. Knopf, 1971.
11. New York: Alfred A. Knopf, 1972.
12. New York: Alfred A. Knopf, 1975.
13. *Too Far To Go: The Maples Stories* (New York: Fawcett, 1979).
14. New York: Alfred A. Knopf, 1976.

CHAPTER EIGHT

1. Kurt Vonnegut, Jr., *Slaughterhouse-Five* (New York: Delacorte Press/Seymour Lawrence, 1969), p. 19.

2. Daniel Okrent, "A Very New Kind of WIR," *Michigan Daily* (Ann Arbor), 21 Jan. 1969, p. 1.

3. Bruce Cook, "When Kurt Vonnegut Talks—And He Does—The Young All Tune In," *National Observer,* 12 Oct. 1970, p. 21; Carol Kramer, "Kurt's College Cult Adopts Him as Literary Guru at 48," *Chicago Tribune,* 15 Nov. 1970, Sec. 5, p. 1; Richard Todd, "The Masks of Kurt Vonnegut, Jr.," *New York Times Magazine,* 24 Jan. 1971, p. 19.

4. Kurt Vonnegut, Jr., *Happy Birthday, Wanda June* (New York: Delacorte Press/Seymour Lawrence, 1971), p. [vii]. Subsequent references to this edition will be indicated parenthetically.

5. Lawrence Mahoney, "Poison Their Minds with Humanity," *Tropic: The Miami Herald Sunday Magazine,* 24 Jan. 1971, p. 10.

6. Loretta McCabe, "An Exclusive Interview with Kurt Vonnegut," *Writer's Yearbook-1970,* p. 104.

7. Vonnegut gives an example in an interview with Carol Troy (*Rags,* Mar. 1971, p. 25): "In my play . . . we have one character who is colonel [*sic*] in the SS, played by Louis Turenne. All through rehearsals he was rehearsing without costume, and then we had a dress rehearsal. It was terrifying . . . everybody was frightened and Louis turned into an utter shit. He wouldn't get off it, wouldn't quit being an SS colonel. We'd chat with Louis and say, 'Hey, that's a swell uniform'—he'd had his hair cut short, too—and we'd try to make jokes with him and just get the most appalling small smiles from him."

8. MS, p. 1, author's corrected typescript, Swen Franklin Parson Library, Northern Illinois University. I am grateful to the Council of Academic Deans of Northern Illinois University for a Research Grant, and to Mr. Clyde Walton, Director of Libraries, for help in obtaining this manuscript.

9. *Slaughterhouse-Five,* p. 17.

10. MS, p. 4.

11. See Jerome Klinkowitz, *The Vonnegut Statement* (New York: Delacorte Press/Seymour Lawrence, 1973).

12. Kurt Vonnegut, *Slapstick* (New York: Delacorte Press/Seymour Lawrence, 1976).

CHAPTER NINE

1. 16 Aug. 1970, p. 15.

2. Donald Barthelme, "Brain Damage," *New Yorker,* 46, 21 Feb. 1970, 42-43. Reprinted with substantial reordering and additions, plus minor stylistic changes, in *City Life* (New York: Farrar, Straus & Giroux, 1970), pp. 131-46. Notes on Barthelme's revisions for all his stories may be found in Jerome Klinkowitz, Asa Pieratt, and Robert Murray Davis, *Donald Barthelme: A Comprehensive Bibliography and Annotated Checklist of Criticism* (Hamden, Conn.: Shoe String Press, 1977).

3. Schickel, p. 42.

4. Alfred Kazin, *Bright Book of Life: American Novelists and Storytellers from Hemingway to Mailer* (Boston: Atlantic Monthly Press/Little, Brown & Co., 1973), p. 273.

5. Kazin, p. 317.

6. William Carlos Williams, "Author's Introduction," *The Wedge* (Cummington, Mass.: Cummington Press, 1944), p. 10.

7. Dick Sutphen, comp. and ed., *Old Engravings and Illustrations: Volume I, People; Volume II, Things* (1965); *Uncensored Situations* and *The Wildest Old Engravings and Illustrations* (both 1966), published in Phoenix by Dick Sutphen Studio.

8. From Barthelme's story "Report," *New Yorker,* 43, 10 June 1967, 34-35. Collected in *Unspeakable Practices, Unnatural Acts* (New York: Farrar, Straus & Giroux, 1968), pp. 49-57.

9. Donald Barthelme, *Guilty Pleasures* (New York: Farrar, Straus & Giroux, 1974), p. [v].

10. "A Nation of Wheels," *New Yorker,* 46, 13 June 1970, 36-39. Collected in *Guilty Pleasures,* pp. 135-45.

11. Another literary artist heavily influenced by twentieth-century painting and collage; see Marjorie Perloff, "Frank O'Hara and the Aesthetics of Attention," *Boundary 2,* 4 (1976), 779-806, and reprinted in Perloff's *Frank O'Hara: Poet Among Painters* (New York: Braziller, 1977).

12. "And Now Let's Hear It for the Ed Sullivan Show!" *Esquire,* 71, Apr. 1969, 126-27, 54, 56. Collected in *Guilty Pleasures,* pp. 101-8.

13. Frank O'Hara, *David Smith: Sculpting Master of Bolton Landing* (New York: WNDT-TV, 1964), cited by Perloff, p. 779.

14. 46 (25 Apr. 1970), 32–33. Collected in *Amateurs* (New York: Farrar, Straus & Giroux, 1976), pp. 115–21. In the collected version Barthelme has changed a few minor references to update the action from the 1960s to the 1970s.

15. Frank O'Hara, "Robert Motherwell," *Art Chronicles 1954–1966* (New York: Venture/Braziller, 1975), pp. 71–72.

16. Donald Barthelme, *Sadness* (New York: Farrar, Straus & Giroux, 1972).

17. Jerome Klinkowitz, "Donald Barthelme [an interview]," *The New Fiction: Interviews with Innovative American Writers,* edited by Joe David Bellamy (Urbana: Univ. of Illinois Press, 1974), p. 49.

18. Donald Barthelme, commentary on "Paraguay," in *Writer's Choice,* ed. Rust Hills (New York: David McKay, 1974), p. 25.

19. Klinkowitz interview, pp. 51–52.

20. Donald Barthelme, et al., "A Symposium on Fiction," *Shenandoah,* 27 (1976), 20–21.

21. Max Ernst, *Une Semaine de Bonté* (New York: Dover, 1976); first published in 1934.

22. Dore Ashton, *A Joseph Cornell Album* (New York: Viking, 1974).

23. Steve Katz, "43," *Moving Parts* (New York: Fiction Collective, 1977), pp. 22–23.

24. For the Cornell Retrospective at the Leo Castelli Gallery (New York) in 1976, Barthelme supplied a catalogue preface in the form of a prose poem, "Cornell." It has been reprinted in *Ontario Review,* 5 (1976–77), p. 50.

EPILOGUE

1. Ronald Sukenick, *Up* (New York: Dial Press, 1968), p. 223.

2. William H. Gass, *Fiction and the Figures of Life* (New York: Knopf, 1970), p. 27.

3. Gilbert Sorrentino, "The Various Isolated: W. C. Williams' Prose," *New American Review,* no. 15 (1972), p. 195.

4. Ronald Sukenick, "Twelve Digressions Toward a Theory of Composition," *New Literary History,* 6 (1974–75), 429–37; "Thirteen Digressions," *Partisan Review,* 43 (1976), 90–101; "Fiction in the Seventies: Ten Digressions on Ten Digressions," *Studies in American Fiction,* 5 (1977), 99–108.

5. Richard Brautigan, *Trout Fishing in America* (San Francisco: Four Seasons Foundation, 1967).

6. Donald Barthelme, "Man's Face," *New Yorker,* 40, 30 May 1964, 29; "Down the Line with the Annual," *New Yorker,* 40, 21 Mar. 1964, 34–35; "L'Lapse," *New Yorker,* 39, 2 Mar. 1963, 29–31; "Snap Snap," *New Yorker,* 41, 28 Aug. 1965, 108–11. The last three parodies are collected in Barthelme's *Guilty Pleasures* (New York: Farrar, Straus & Giroux, 1974).

7. Donald Barthelme, *Snow White* (New York: Atheneum, 1967).

8. Donald Barthelme, "Report," *Unspeakable Practices, Unnatural Acts* (New York: Farrar, Straus & Giroux, 1968), p. 55.

9. Donald Barthelme, *Great Days* (New York: Farrar, Straus & Giroux, 1979).

10. Walter Abish, *Alphabetical Africa* (New York: New Directions, 1974).

11. Gilbert Sorrentino, *The Sky Changes* (New York: Hill & Wang, 1966); *Steelwork* (New York: Pantheon, 1970).

12. Gilbert Sorrentino, *Imaginative Qualities of Actual Things* (New York: Pantheon, 1971).

13. Gilbert Sorrentino, *Splendide-Hotel* (New York: New Directions, 1973).

14. Gilbert Sorrentino, *Mulligan Stew* (New York: Grove Press, 1979).

15. Raymond Federman, *Double or Nothing* (Chicago: Swallow Press, 1971).

16. Ronald Sukenick, *Out* (Chicago: Swallow Press, 1973).

17. Raymond Federman, *Take It or Leave It* (New York: Fiction Collective, 1976).

18. Clarence Major, *Reflex and Bone Structure* (New York: Fiction Collective, 1974).

19. Clarence Major, *Emergency Exit* (New York: Fiction Collective, 1979).

20. Raymond Federman, *Surfiction* (Chicago: Swallow Press, 1975).

21. John Gardner, *On Moral Fiction* (New York: Basic Books, 1978).

22. William Kotzwinkle, *The Fan Man* (New York: Avon, 1974).

23. Tom Robbins, *Another Roadside Attraction* (New York: Doubleday, 1971).

24. Tom Robbins, *Even Cowgirls Get the Blues* (Boston: Houghton Mifflin, 1976).

25. Rob Swigart, *Little America, A.K.A. /A Cosmic Fable,* and *The Time Trip* (Boston: Houghton Mifflin, respectively 1977, 1978, 1979).

26. Gerald Rosen, *Blues for a Dying Nation* (New York: Dial Press, 1972).

27. Gerald Rosen, *The Carmen Miranda Memorial Flagpole* (San Rafael, Calif.: Presidio Press, 1977).

28. Gerald Rosen, *Dr. Ebenezer's Book & Liquor Store* (New York: St. Martin's Press, 1980).

I N D E X

Page numbers for major discussions are in italics.

DATE DUE			